You may contact Ms. Keller at:
Mary Lou Keller
PMB #155
2370 West Highway 89A, Suite 11
Sedona, Arizona 86336-5349

Echoes of Sedona Past

Dear Reader:
Hope you enjoy my book.
Blessings,
Mary Lou Keller

Mary Lou Keller

Cover and artwork by Diana Morro

ISBN 1-891824-23-6

Contents

Preface

The birth of this book was not easy for me. Without the loving and dedicated efforts of two dear friends, it never could have reached fruition.

I had no intention of writing a book, but for several years I wrote monthly articles and stories that were published in the wonderful *Sedona Journal of Emergence*. They were well received; however, as time went on I found it harder and harder to meet my deadline, and finally I stopped writing.

When my artist niece Diana Morro (a portrait painter of Indian children) and many other friends began urging me to write my stories for a book, I resisted, insisting that many good books were on the market and wondering what I could possibly write that was important enough to publish.

Then I had a fascinating reading from Kadea, a psychic reader who lived in Sedona at the time. She told me that I absolutely must write a book about my memories of early Sedona. "If you pass on and leave your stories untold," she said, "they will be lost forever."

After giving thought to her words, I began to see that she was right. Maybe I should be taking this book idea more seriously. After all, if I gathered together all the stories I had already written, I would have a running start on a book. So finally I decided to give it a try.

Diana was delighted with my decision and tried to help by giving me three hand-held audio-cassette recorders (one for my car, one for her car and one for my bedroom). She told me that talking my stories into the recorder would be much easier than writing them down.

I admit I was having difficulty with my writing, because I was almost too ill and incapacitated to do it. Talking into a recorder sounded like a good idea and works well for many people, but it didn't work for me. Many times I tried to talk into the recorders, but for some reason everything I tried to say just stopped, froze and refused to flow. Eventually my frustration overwhelmed me and I gave up on the recorders.

As I lay awake one night, listening to the memories that flooded into my head, I remembered I had started writing when I was only five, writing always in the middle of the night. Perhaps that was the way I could write now — at night when the words poured out so smoothly. So I captured a few stories on paper before a couple of strokes and several other mishaps slowed me down. I lost my energy for writing and once again was ready to let go the entire project.

At this point, at the gentle urging of my writer friend, Charmaine Boericke, I began telling my stories to her. She would write down my words, partly in shorthand and partly in longhand, and transcribe them later. Many afternoons we met together for several hours while I told my stories and she listened and wrote. We did lots of our work on the phone too, and in this way the pages of manuscript began to pile up. We were making progress.

During this phase I again began to awaken at 2:30 or 3:00 in the early mornings, and I did my best to scribble down the stories that tumbled into my memory. Charmaine managed to read my handwriting (which really was quite dreadful) and wrote the stories down for me. This method worked so well that I was encouraged to continue, and we spent hours going over the material together. She was simply great at interpreting my efforts and writing everything into a legible manuscript.

Once again we were back in business.

When the time came for the handwritten pages to be typed, we handed them over to another very wonderful long-time friend, Marjorie McEwen, who is an experienced and excellent typist and on good terms with her computer. We three worked beautifully together, and now Charmaine and I began to see that the collection of stories and articles was starting to take shape. Even though both of us were getting on in years (and at times were not feeling very energetic), we managed to create the manuscript.

Without Charmaine's support and enthusiasm for the project, I know this book would never have been written. She was an unfailing source of inspiration and expertise in organizing and editing my material. I could not have done it without her.

And Marjorie's professional skill in rapidly turning out pages and pages of typed manuscript has been a blessing! Without these loyal and caring friends, this book would not have made it. I shall be forever grateful for their help and thank them from my heart.

Thanks also go to Mary Marla McNeil, whom I have known for years and who is a close friend of Diana's. In the earliest days of discussing the possibility of this book, she was instrumental in helping me get started by typing some of my first published stories. This work was interrupted by her previous commitments to civic duties and to her clients.

I truly thank the many other friends who constantly encouraged me and showed interest in my stories. They helped me stay on track.

Special thanks go to my niece Diana, who never failed to cheer me on when I wavered. She always knew I could do it and, with help, I did it . . .

Shortly before this book went to press a friend suggested that I give serious thought to changing my title from Echoes of Sedona Past to Memories of Sedona Past.

I wasn't really thrilled with this idea but wondered if the change had value. So I phoned Charmaine and asked her what she thought.

She made no comment for a long moment. "You really want to know?"

I assured her that I definitely did want her opinion. After a brief pause she said, "Let me think about it. I'll call you back."

A couple of hours later she faxed me a most interesting answer to my question. It was so beautifully expressed, I decided to add it here — just as she wrote it in her wonderful stylized handwriting.

Here is an exact copy of this most intriguing fax:

Mary Lou ---   re: title of book   6/26/99

ECHOES of SEDONA PAST

vs

MEMORIES of SEDONA PAST

Echoes is more subtle, delicate and elusive than Memories. Echoes hints at keen insight and spiritual reflections.

Echoes is more romantic, more unusual and more catchy; it promises more of inner investigation, and it implies a depth and breadth not necessarily found in Memories which usually is more a reporting from recall.

Memories (like a photograph) describes the scene but lacks the artistic and expansive flavor of Echoes.

There is a sense of poetry in Echoes. Memories is more unimaginative and prosaic.

Echoes is kind of mysterious and implies something more than a Memory. It opens up a sense of wonder!

cl

Foreword

Sedona, Arizona, has always been an unusual place, blessed by the energy of its strikingly beautiful natural setting and its historical legacy as holy ground. Over the years, as if drawn by a giant magnet, many people have been attracted to Sedona — living, dreaming and being unusual.

Over forty years ago when Mary Lou Keller and her husband Glenn discovered Sedona, it was a small village of about 2500 inhabitants, mostly ranchers, retirees, artists and business people. At that time Sedona was pretty much a secret. Few people had heard of it, and if they had looked for it on a map, they would not have found it. Sedona was not a place you simply happened upon on your way to somewhere; you had to detour to reach it.

From Flagstaff you would go out of your way, driving some thirty miles south on a narrow mountain road, steep of grade, with incredibly sharp curves, turns and switchbacks. All the while you would be bombarded from all sides by views of red cliffs, startling rock formations, forest vistas, meadows of wildflowers in their season and the flowing waters of the unpredictable Oak Creek, which can be pastorally serene or wildly chaotic, depending on early spring snowfall in the mountains.

Long ago, when only Native Americans knew this spectacular high-desert country, they considered this valley of red rock spires, energy vortexes and mysterious hidden canyons to be sacred ground. It seems this mystique still lingers over Sedona, for among the approximately four million tourists who visit here during a single year, many will return on a spiritual vision quest. Numerous people who now live here will tell you that Sedona has totally enchanted and bewitched them and they cannot stay away.

Since the 1920s when Hollywood discovered Sedona, the population and size of the village have grown constantly. But as recently as ten years ago, you would have found only one stoplight, no streetlights and no neon signs (even on storefronts) to obscure the starry nights. Also no sidewalks, no fast foods, no shopping centers, no time-shares and almost no traffic. The **Flicker Shack** was the only movie house in town, and the streets were nearly deserted after the sun went down.

Even today, tumbleweeds still bounce down the lanes, coyotes may amble along the street in broad daylight and packs of javelinas (native wild pigs) will be delighted to ruin your newly planted garden in the dead of night. And yes, the sky still seems bluer, the air fresher and the sun brighter as it reflects off crimson rock sculptures that shimmer and shift with every passing cloud.

Just as many had done before, and still do, Mary Lou Keller fell in love with Sedona at first sight. "This is home," she announced. It would be eight and a half years after her discovery before she and her husband moved from Oregon to Sedona. However, because they had visited the area every winter to explore, by the time they moved they felt much at home. And home it has been to this very day.

Recognizing the enormous potential of the area, the Kellers became involved with real estate and opened the successful Keller Realty. Mary Lou Keller is considered the oldest working broker in Sedona. An honorary plaque has been presented to her in recognition of her forty-two years in real estate. Today, hundreds of residents will tell you that Mary Lou was the first person they met in Sedona. Ask her if she knows so-and-so, and she is likely to answer, "Oh, yes. I sold them their first home when they moved here."

However, real estate was not Mary Lou's only interest. She was deeply involved with spiritual growth and higher consciousness. She started the first metaphysical church in Sedona, which she called **The Sedona Church of Light**. It was through her church that she met and brought to Sedona so many of the famous spiritual leaders, healers and gurus of the time, often housing them in her own home. Her open, questioning mind and sincere search for truth in all things have attracted to her (and to Sedona) an amazing number of unusual speakers and teachers from other cultures as well as her own. These were creative people, people who walked their own path, danced to their own music and followed the voice of spirit and of their hearts.

Today, Mary Lou's phone rings constantly. Old friends, new friends of all ages and people she has never met call to touch base; draw from her knowledge; ask her out to lunch or to speak at some event or appear in a TV documentary; or just bask in the light and joy of her being.

Mary Lou Keller is a natural-born storyteller, and her *Echoes of Sedona Past* is a collection of true stories about the unusual people and events that are part of an almost forgotten historical record of Sedona. This insightfully written book sparks memories of small-town growth and development and introduces colorful characters who contributed so much spice to the reputation of this unique and beautiful town.

She allows us to peek into Sedona's early days of East

Indian gurus and psychic healers and takes us along with her on a holy pilgrimage to India with Indian royalty. This trip is a journey of surprises. She tells of horseback travel in the high Himalayas, of menacing Sikh warriors and of her meeting with the Keeper of the Akashic Records, whose son, several years later, comes to Sedona to bring her a message.

Always aware of her personal spiritual journey, Mary Lou writes of spiritual lessons learned and insights gained during her adventurous and productive eighty-five years. Her main purpose in life is to open minds, and this she has done and is still doing. Today she continues her eternal search for natural healing and knowledge of life and she never, never ceases to learn and to grow. Many of these stories originally appeared in the popular *Sedona Journal of Emergence,* which is published by O'Ryin Swanson of Light Technology Publishing and has national as well as worldwide distribution.

As you read these echoes of Mary Lou Keller's memories of Sedona, of the unusual people and unusual happenings she recalls from years gone by, you cannot escape being fascinated by the author. And, no doubt, you will agree that Mary Lou Keller herself is one of Sedona's most unusual people, a shining treasure living in this blessed and most unusual place.

Charmaine Boericke

Author's Note to Readers

As I gather together my stories for *Echoes of Sedona Past*, I realize how deeply my childhood experiences and circumstances influenced my life and how they molded my attitudes, wishes and dreams. This is how it all began:

I was born October 17, 1914, with the name Mary Louise Chantler. My parents were not at all compatible, and even as a child this disharmony caused me great emotional stress. Once when I was eighteen months old and starting to walk, I took my mother's hand and led her to my father, placing her hand in his and looking up at them, wondering why they did not love each other.

Perhaps as a sensitive child I was so overwhelmed by the family discord that unconsciously my body reacted. Perhaps the constant conflict between my parents could be the reason I've had asthma since a very early age. Doctors today do not know much more about asthma than they did eighty years ago, except now they prescribe all kinds of drugs and steroids that relieve the symptoms but have many side effects and do not cure. I know, because I've tried these things. Today many alternative healers suggest that asthma is rooted in severe emotional trauma. I strongly suspect they are right.

Over my long lifetime, half of which I've spent in Sedona, I've searched for the answers to *why* I have asthma and how can I cure myself. At first I thought of asthma as my curse, but as I grew into more wisdom, I saw that actually it has been a blessing. Because I continually asked *why*, I was propelled to look for answers that drew me into a variety of studies. I studied diet, health, mind control, philosophy, psychology and anything else I could find relating to health of body, mind and spirit. I actually used myself as my own research laboratory. Through this search for health I discovered many answers, but I never successfully found the answer to my cure along the way. I'm still searching . . .

When I was very young, my mother taught me to read. Each week she would go to the library and get seven books for me, and I read a book a day. By the time I entered high school I had read most of the reading required for my age. By the time I was five, I was reading to a group of children in the neighborhood, drawing pictures and writing poetry. I always took a pad and pencil to bed with me because I was awakened about two or three in the morning with poetry pouring out of me, and I had to write it down or I could not go back to sleep. The poems were deep and philosophical, and often I did not understand them. I have wondered many times since where those words and ideas came from. Mother saved my poetry for years, but finally, after many moves, it was lost.

Since my mother had to work to help support the family, I was left alone in bed most of the time — trying to breathe, or just survive. I went to school when I was able, and when I was not able, school chums would bring the assignments to me and I would send them back the next morning. Many of my grade school teachers were irritated with me because they didn't recognize my illness and thought I was looking for attention. I actually had to quit the first grade because my teacher made my life miserable, which, of course, made my asthma worse. (In later years an x-ray revealed that I also had tuberculosis.)

Because I was alone so much and couldn't take part
in activities most children were involved in, I became a
quiet and introverted little person. My sister and
brother, both younger than I, were normal, healthy children and had no understanding of my dilemma. My sister, who was three years younger, thought I was being fa-
vored and pampered, so she began a lifetime of
resentment toward me.

Often I was so weak I couldn't walk, and I remember
crawling on my hands and knees down a hallway that
seemed endless, stopping to lie on the floor to rest until
I had enough energy to crawl a little farther to the bathroom. At night mother put me in a big chair in the living room to sleep, because at times I could not breathe
lying flat. She really did not expect me to survive. I was
a great worry to her, but somehow my health problems
seemed to build an inner strength that later served me
well. I just kept on going and doing what I could, refusing to let it crush my spirit. I learned to live in my
books and thoughts instead of physical action. I believe
that if I had been strong and well, I would have been a
dancer or an athlete, because I had a great admiration
and desire for those activities.

My mother was a wonderful mother who often enter-
tained us children by playing the harmonica while dancing a jig. Mother also allowed us to dig a big hole in the
back yard, which we filled with water. It was a great
muddy swimming hole that all the children in the
neighborhood enjoyed. I don't know what the parents
thought, but we loved it. I imagined all mothers did
such things, and I was very surprised when I learned
they didn't. Mother often took us and the neighbor
children to a park a few blocks from where we lived, and
we had a wonderful time. She also let us have all kinds

of pets: dogs, cats, ducks, chickens, rabbits, and at one time even a lamb. I realized later that my father allowed this only because he knew some of our pets would wind up on the table for Sunday dinner.

I had a pet chicken named Tilly who rode around on my shoulder and clucked into my ear. When Tilly appeared on the Sunday dinner table, I refused to eat her. I told my father I could not eat my friend. He took off his belt and gave me a sound thrashing, but I was stubborn and refused to eat Tilly. Perhaps that is one reason I do not like eating meat, although later I found I had lived many lives in India, so it was natural for me to be a vegetarian.

Another strong memory of my father is when he took us for Sunday afternoon car rides. We rode in a touring car enclosed by some sort of isinglass windows, and he smoked cigars, which made me very ill. He would have to stop the car so I could get out and up-chuck, which made him really angry. He would take off his belt and give me a whipping for being sick. My father had a terrible temper and often whipped me. I was afraid of him.

When I was about nine, my parents separated. Mother was so frightened of him, she fled with us children to Waitsburg, Washington, where we were close to her family. I think she must have been terribly upset emotionally, because she left us with different members of the family. My sister and brother were placed in Walla Walla, whereas I was sent to live with my aunt and uncle on a large sheep ranch near Dayton, Washington.

I loved the rural life. It was the most interesting part of my childhood, and I have many happy memories of the two years I spent there, going to a little red schoolhouse where I was the only girl among eleven ranch boys. The teacher was delighted to have a girl in her class and taught me all kinds of little dances. I especially remember the Highland fling. Another clear memory of those school days is the time I stepped out the door and encountered a huge rattlesnake curled up on the step.

Every day was a bright new adventure for me. I rode Nellie, my uncle's horse, the two and a half miles to school — except in the springtime when she had to pull the plough. On those days I walked to and from school. Either way, walking or riding in the early mornings was a wonderful experience. There were meadowlarks singing from fence posts, little wild rabbits and squirrels scurrying about and wildflowers for me to stop and smell.

Nellie was a special friend, allowing me to ride her frontways, sideways, backwards or standing on her back. In those days I didn't even have a saddle. When I fell off, she would stop immediately and not move her feet until I had climbed back on. Sometimes, because I was enjoying myself so much, I lost track of the time and had to take a shortcut and swim Nellie across the river so I wouldn't be late for school. I just put my feet up on her neck and hung onto her mane. What fun and magical memories!

My uncle's ranch was a large one where he raised 5000 or more sheep for market. A railroad track ran right through the ranch, for loading the sheep on their way to Chicago. Spring loading was a dreadful time for me. I hated to see the sheep go away, even though I wasn't told what was to become of them. It was especially sad because I adopted all the orphaned lambs and they thought I was their mother. I put the baby lambs to bed in boxes behind the wood-burning stove in the kitchen and fed them milk from a beer bottle with a nipple on it.

One year I raised nine lambs. When they were grown and had rejoined the herd, they would break away from the flock and run to me if I were in sight. More than once they knocked me down and walked all over me in their exuberance to greet their "mom." When they were about one year old and market time came, I begged my uncle not to send my lambs away. My uncle said, "A sheep is a sheep," and off they went, leaving a broken-hearted little girl behind. What a flood of memories I have of my childhood on that sheep ranch, and I enjoy writing about them.

Today I do most of my writing from about 2:30 to 4:30 in the morning. Words just come tumbling out, and I have to turn on the light and start recording ideas and memories as fast as I can write. This is the same way I wrote my poetry when I was a child, only then I wrote in the dark, because to turn on a light would have disturbed my sister and brother, who slept in the same room. In the morning it was difficult to figure out what I had written because the words were often written on top of each other. I also wrote poetry in high school, some of which I still possess. Whenever anyone would ask me what I was going to be when I grew up, I would promptly say "a writer." In my early thirties I wrote fiction stories and once submitted them to an editor who sent them back, commenting that they were good but that I should wait until I was older and had my own experiences to write about.

So now at eighty-five, that is exactly what I am doing — writing about my own experiences, and at this age I certainly have plenty to write about. I find it easy to write what I have lived, and I have done a lot of living.

Echoes of Sedona Past

PART ONE

Early Days in Sedona

Glenn and Mary Lou Keller with Cisco and Poncho.

1

How I Discovered Sedona

There is always a beginning to every story, so I will begin my story by telling you how I discovered Sedona.

It all started about fifty years ago when my beloved stepdaughter was diagnosed with carcinoma in her left hip joint. This cancer can grow rapidly in a young body, and our Judy was only ten.

Glenn and I were told she had about six months to live and that her hip and leg should be removed — an operation she might not survive. The doctors said we were playing God when we refused the operation and took her back home to Sandy, Oregon. Meanwhile, another little girl with the same problem as Judy's died after this same operation.

In spite of our vigorous search for healing, nothing worked, and helplessly we were watching her fade away. Then we heard of the Hoxsey cure. Because the AMA and FDA would not allow Hoxsey to send his medicine through the mail, we would have to go to his clinic in Texas to get it. But Judy was too weak to make the trip. Then, as if by magic, a bottle of the Hoxsey medicine was given to us along with directions for taking it and a special diet.

We started the treatment immediately, and in two weeks Judy's pain was gone and she began to thrive. A miracle was happening before our eyes! In a year she was strong enough to make the trip, and the three of us took off for the Hoxsey Cancer Clinic in Houston.

Today Judy is about sixty years old, the picture of vibrant health. A cheerful and positive person, she has married twice and lives her life with a captivating sense of true joy. Her crutch has not slowed her down nor kept her from a successful career.

In a strange, convoluted way, our desperate search for Judy's healing led us to the red rock country. Indeed, God works in wondrous ways. It so happened that as we drove home from the clinic (with a year's supply of Hoxsey's medicine), we stopped for dinner in Flagstaff, Arizona. It was Thanksgiving Day, and we truly had a special reason to be thankful that year.

Leaving Flagstaff, we took a detour on Oak Creek Canyon Road to enjoy the amazing scenery we had heard about. After a breathtaking forty-five minute drive, we found Sedona and were enchanted, just as so many people are today. We moved here permanently forty-two years ago, and here I have grown in spirituality, learned important lessons, found many friends, enjoyed a successful career and been nourished by the

4

mystique of this beautiful area and the fascinating people I've been fortunate enough to meet.

So this is the story of how I discovered this magical village and felt I had truly come home. Although Sedona is no longer a tiny village, it is still magical, and even after all these years I would not want to live anywhere else in the world.

First Movie House

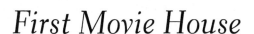

*M*any residents who have lived in Sedona less than ten years cannot possibly imagine what it was like in the 1950s. When I first visited Sedona more than forty-eight years ago, there were only about 2500 people living here, and the old uptown area (which is now tourist land) was a small village consisting of a bank, post office, grocery store, drugstore, gas station, tavern, a couple of restaurants and six motel units. There were also two real estate offices. (Glenn and I started a third.) It was pretty much a complete little town, all within a few blocks. Almost everyone was able to walk from home to any place of business.

There was no parking problem in those days. Some farmers and ranchers came to town in their trucks or on horseback, but there were very few tourists because Sedona was not even on the map, and those who wanted to come here had difficulty finding it. Sedona had not been discovered by the outside world, and trying to make a living was a real problem. Now it seems that the whole world is aware of this area and is making fast tracks to get here.

We had no movie theater, and at six o'clock the radio station shut the wattage down and we could get only static. Unless you had a very powerful radio that could get outside stations, you were out of luck for news and entertainment. Of course, at that time television was just a dream.

The local uptown tavern was the only place in town where we might find sociability or music. Occasionally on weekends a wandering musician would show up at the tavern. There was a roadhouse three miles west of town on 89A called **Rainbow's End** where we could get something to eat, have a drink, play pool and often dance on Saturday nights. Rainbow's End is one of the few restaurants to survive over the years. Way back then there was nothing on 89A all the way from uptown to the roadhouse except tumbleweeds, grasshoppers and jackrabbits.

A few years later Don Pratt, who had once owned the Crystal Ballroom in Los Angeles but was now a local realtor and musician, got a group of musicians together. They played wonderful dance music, and we had a stomping good time.

A special treat was the Museum Club in Flagstaff on old Route 66. On occasion we would go up there to have dinner and dance, but mostly to watch the action which was real Old West at its rowdy best. It was so wild, there was always a sheriff with gun on hip standing at the door ready to quell any trouble, and there was always plenty of trouble. The club was frequented mostly by cowboys and Indians (I am not kidding), and a wild bunch they were. The cowboys looked like they had just come off the range, with their hats on and manure on their boots, and they were well liquored up.

The dancing was about the wildest I had ever seen. If a cowboy asked a girl to dance and she said no, she was literally picked up and dumped on the dance floor, and she would dance whether she wanted to or not. It was not a place to go unescorted, that's for sure. The Indians were also in their cups, and this is when the fights started between the cowboys and Indians. It was quite obvious they were not fond of each other.

The Museum Club had actually been an old museum, hence the name. It was really a unique building, made of logs. Inside you could see that the roof was held up by trees complete with branches, and in the branches were stuffed owls, birds and animals. It was so dark inside that it took awhile to get used to the twilight so you could see this menagerie. Mostly college kids go there now.

Some of us Sedonans got our heads together and decided to make our own entertainment. Whenever the old Sedona Lodge (where the **Circle K** and the **King's Ransom** are now) was not being occupied by movie companies on location, we would rent the old building they used for a sound stage and storage. Then we would rent one of the movies filmed in Sedona and, with a home projector, rig up our own movie house. People brought their own chairs and we hung a large sheet on the wall and sat back to enjoy the show.

This building was right next to the stables where horses were kept. As the cowboys and Indians galloped across the sheet, if we took a deep breath we could smell the pungent odor of horse manure. It gave a bit of reality to our movie. We called our primitive little movie house "The Smellorama." This was the first movie house in Sedona. It was great fun, and a memory I will always cherish.

3

First Jazz on the Rocks

We early Sedonans, always ready for evening entertainment, put together some wonderful evenings in the back country with a potluck supper and hamburgers grilled over an open fire. Another realtor and my husband and I organized the cookouts by inviting any newcomers in town, some of the old-timers and maybe a couple of ministers to help everyone get acquainted. We shuttled the gang by jeep to our rendezvous because the places we selected were impossible to get to by car. Most of these wonderful places have been closed off by the Forest Service, so these days the only way to get to them would be by walking.

Bill Larock, a member of our group, had a gasoline generator, and he would bring his stereo and go early to position his speakers in strategic locations, often climbing a cliff to place them. We called him our Music Man. He had a wonderful collection of dance music on big, round tapes. (This was long before tape cassettes.)

We always chose a fairly smooth spot where we could dance in the moonlight. So we had the very first Jazz on the Rocks.

We would build a bonfire (another thing you would not dare do now), get the music going and set out the food. On one occasion Don Pratt, who was the cook, found we had forgotten a spatula to turn the burgers. He rummaged around in his jeep and pulled out a small shovel. (Most jeep drivers carried one.) He wiped it off saying, "Don't worry, folks. I only use it to shovel manure." We laughingly called our burgers "shovel burgers."

4

First Shopping Center

hen we first arrived, Glenn loved Sedona as much as I did, but he had some disappointing experiences in the real estate business. Glenn was a visionary and could see what Sedona needed for development, but often he was thwarted in his attempts to bring his creative vision to fruition. One project worked out beautifully, though. He and I made a good team, and together we made it happen.

Sedona had a bad eyesore in a most obvious and strategic location at the intersection of Highway 89A and Jordan Road. An old barn stood there, which was unsightly enough, but the old cars and farm machinery that cluttered up the lot made the place an unsightly mess. The man who owned the barn and property was a mechanic, and those broken-down relics were things he expected to repair someday.

Glenn came up with an exciting idea for improving that corner and upgrading the entire area. Good at me-

Mary Lou, Glenn and saleperson in front of our
new real estate office attached to an old barn.

chanical drawing, he drew a sketch to show how he
would like to see that lot look. He drew the barn as part
of a small shopping center, and on the corner of the lot
he sketched a small building with a sign KELLER RE-
ALTY prominently displayed. It really looked great. He
and I agreed to concentrate on his sketch, and every
time we passed that corner, we projected this image of
the shopping center in our minds and imagined we saw
our real estate sign on our office as though it were already a reality. We did this faithfully for several
months.

In the meantime, Glenn went about getting to know
the fellow who owned the place. It turned out that this
man was suspicious of strangers, especially real estate
people, so it was a slow process for Glenn to become acquainted with him, but eventually they became friendly.
When Glenn would ask him if he would consider selling
the lot, the answer always was a resounding NO.

However, as time went by, the owner changed his mind and told Glenn what he would take for the property, but he would not sign a listing or pay a commission. Many old-timers had that same attitude, so Glenn proceeded to search for someone who could see the possibilities of a small shopping center on that corner.

He found just such a person, who agreed to build a small office for us (attached to the south side of the barn), and he gave us three years free rent for our commission. It all worked out and eventually did become exactly what Glenn and I had projected for that area.

Our office was built first, and we occupied it for several years. At that time it was the best location in town for a real estate office. Sometimes it was difficult to get our work done because we were besieged constantly by visitors stopping by to chat, ask directions or ask where there was a good place to eat and so on.

The barn was converted into a large room with a cement floor and was leased to a person who put on square dances. Gradually, as the little complex grew, a walk-through was added, with little shops on each side. This was Sedona's first shopping center. I remember a small bakery run by a baker and his wife — she, by the way, still lives in Sedona.

5

A View for the Church of the Red Rocks

nother project Glenn accomplished, with patience and foresight, was locating the property for the **Church of the Red Rocks**. A group from that church asked him to find a high spot with a super view. He found the perfect location at the high point of a new subdivision called **Broken Arrow**; however, a few lots had already been sold and a house had been built on one of them. Also, the subdivision was *not* zoned for a church. Glenn would have to get the consent of every lot owner in order for the church to be built there, so he set about to accomplish this by way of letters and phone calls.

Glenn worked on this for a year and almost got it all together. But there was one holdout. The people who had built their winter home on one of the lots lived in the East, and they refused to comply. So Glenn patiently pursued them by letters and phone calls, and at last they agreed.

So the beautiful Church of the Red Rocks was built and still stands there in its magnificent setting with its super-glorious view.

When Glenn decided that what West Sedona needed was a golf course, he gradually put together a group of tracts that had not yet been developed. It took awhile, but he finally got all the owners to agree to sell at a certain price per acre, and it looked as if Sedona would have a golf course. But one of the tracts held out for more money than had originally been agreed upon, so there went that dream right down the drain. A few other of his plans had a similar ending, and he began to be a bit disillusioned with Sedona real estate.

At this time he became restless and tried to talk me into moving to Hawaii. I was extremely involved with many projects and felt that I had a destiny in Sedona. I simply could not consent to leaving. One morning over the breakfast table we discussed our differences and decided it was only fair for each of us to do what we most wanted to do. After twenty-two years of a good marriage, we shook hands like the good friends we were and he went to Hawaii.

At first I found it very difficult to keep my office functioning without him. I was also lonely; we really missed each other. He would occasionally come home to visit for a month or two, and once in a while I would visit him in Hawaii. Eventually we realized that this arrangement was not really working, so we got a friendly divorce.

We are still the very best of friends.

6

Realtors, Developers and Our Haunted House

ealtors and developers just can't leave Sedona alone. Today the competition among real estate agencies is fierce. As the native trees and land are cleared for more and more building, I often wish that Sedona had become a national park long before houses and condominiums started creeping up and down the hills and valleys.

There were those who pushed the national park idea, but they were overruled and Sedona continues to grow like Topsy. Forest lands we once considered safe are constantly being traded and sold. Housing developments and time-shares mushroom, then old roads are widened and new roads are built to help accommodate the heavy traffic. Already the demand on the sewer system has surpassed its intended capacity and some people worry about the water supply. Growth and high prices seem inevitable.

Forty years ago all was not that great with the developers, either. One developer tried changing the name of Grasshopper Flats to Rainbow Valley, trying to make the lots more attractive to buyers. It sounded very nice, but when you mentioned Rainbow Valley, people would say, "Oh, you mean Grasshopper Flats." The new name didn't take, so Grasshopper Flats is still with us.

One realtor would drive his clients up to Panorama Vista on Airport Hill, where the building lots had red rock views and were more expensive than those on the flats. The clients, of course, would fall in love with the view and say, "Oh, this is wonderful! We'll take this lot." Back to the office they'd go, sign the papers and go home happy. When they came back to build their new home, they'd find they owned a lot in Grasshopper Flats, with no view. There were many bitter legal hassles over this kind of treatment.

This same realtor caused the murder and suicide of the couple who owned the building that Glenn and I purchased later, which became known as the Keller Building. it stood on the site of today's beautiful **Hillside Court** and parking lot and was my second home in Sedona.

Busy as this realtor was with selling lots and being sued, he was also busy playing around with several lonely widows in town. He started romancing the wife of the man who owned the building we would buy later. The owner of this building was an architect, and business was not going too well. He became deeply depressed and probably wasn't paying enough attention to his wife. When some friends told him that this real estate man was "entertaining" his wife, he saw red.

That night he grabbed his gun and went out looking

for the realtor. He couldn't find him, so he went back home, found his wife asleep in bed and shot her. Then he killed himself. The next morning, their three teen-age boys found their mother and father both dead.

Because of this double tragedy, nobody wanted the building, and it stood empty for a long time. When Glenn and I bought it we had to remove the blood-soaked carpet in the bedroom and plug up the bullet hole in the wall above the headboard. The distraught husband must have missed his first shot.

Glenn Keller in front of our first
real estate office on Highway 179.

"Why did you buy that house with all its bad vibes?" people asked.

"We're going to make it a happy house," I would an-swer. In those days I didn't believe in ghosts.

So we moved in and set about creating our happy house. But it wasn't all that easy. At night my beagle, Pico (her name should have been Poco, but I didn't learn her gender 'til too late), would lie in the hall outside the bedroom door, growling deep in her throat, hair standing on end. I wondered why she acted like that until I realized that she saw something I didn't. Visiting psychics who came to the house would say, "Oh, my! What happened here? A terrible, terrible tragedy!"

I was convinced my house was haunted, so I asked for advice and read about clearing my house of unwanted energies. I was determined to handle the problem myself. I played my "Purple Flame" record over and over. (It was supposed to heal negativity.) I burned incense and I lit candles, but nothing helped. Finally I had to get assistance from friends who knew more about getting rid of ghosts than I did.

Mary Lou and Pico in her turquoise jeep.

One day she caught a rabbit and brought it back to show me. Gently she put it down and stood there licking it, looking up at me as if to say, "Hey! I caught it. Now what do I do?" Finally the stupefied rabbit regained its senses and hopped away. Pico made no effort to chase it, but watched with mild interest until it vanished in the brush.

I often drove myself out on the jeep trail just to sit and meditate. This was before tourists began to come and go on the trail, when it was still a peaceful, quiet place. Sometimes I would receive inspiration for my Sunday sermons as I sat there in the serenity of the high-desert wilderness.

One day the wind was blowing hard and I was enjoying watching the trees as they danced in the gale. I noticed the saplings would bend almost to the ground and the "teen-agers" halfway over in the high wind. But the older trees stood steady and strong, with only the tips of their branches moving a little. I used this observation as a basis for my next sermon, showing that youth can be almost bowled over yet still recover from the storms of life, while age gains strength and wisdom, no longer being so deeply affected by the turmoil that life brings.

It just happened that a lady in the congregation brought her minister brother to church with her that Sunday. He was so impressed that he used the theme of my sermon for one of his services at his church in California. His sister told me about it later.

My little turquoise jeep and I had great times together driving here, there and everywhere. We were a familiar sight around Sedona — the bright turquoise jeep with Pico prancing on its hood, and me dressed like a turquoise cowgirl in turquoise hat, turquoise boots, turquoise everything.

One time an old friend of Glenn's came to visit. Glenn had to go out of town, so he asked me to show his friend the sights. That day I was wearing a black lace dress and high-heeled patent-leather pumps. I told the friend if he'd wait while I changed my clothes, I'd drive him out on our jeep trail. He said he'd hate to miss it, but he was on such a tight schedule he didn't have time to wait for me to change. I kicked off my pumps and said, "Let's go," and off we went in my jeep. He insisted on taking pictures so he could prove to his friends back home that he really did take a jeep tour with a barefoot lady driver who wore a black lace dress.

Glenn and I went on enjoying our jeep trail and our

tours. One day Don Pratt said to Glenn, "Why don't you start a jeep tour business?" And Glenn said, "No, I wouldn't want to do that. I only enjoy driving out there when I want to. If I did it as a steady thing, it would take all the fun out of it for me." So Don Pratt said, "Would you mind if *I* do it?" And that is how the **Pink Jeep Tour** got started.

All this was years ago, and now Sedona has many jeep trails with red jeeps, pink jeeps and other jeeps touring up and down the back country in all directions, carrying excited tourists to see the views, observe archaeological sites, take pictures and visit vortexes. Jeep tours are one of our most popular tourist attractions.

8

Pioneers and Outlaws

*J*oe and Mary Hancock were early pioneers in this red rock country. They lived out on their ranch near Loy Butte, twenty-one miles from Sedona. They were our oldest friends, wonderful, salt-of-the-earth Arizonans. They had met in Jerome and later moved out to their ranch, where they have lived at least sixty-five years, running a few cattle and keeping a large vineyard.

The Hancocks were the kind of people who never met a stranger and were friendly to anyone who went out to the ranch to see the Indian ruins and petroglyphs on the canyon walls and rocks. Over the years, we learned a lot from the Hancocks about early Sedona and even herded cattle out there during spring and fall roundups.

In those days outlaws roamed the back country. as did cattle rustlers, who often herded their stolen cattle down toward Mexico where they were sold over the border. Many times these men would stop at the ranch and were welcomed, fed and given a place to sleep just like any other visitor. No one was ever turned away.

"Where you from, stranger?" was not an appropriate question in those days, although Western movies might lead you to think otherwise. No one was asked his name or where he came from, because it was likely he was on the lam. Asking too many questions might get you shot. That's how it was in those good old days!

Joe passed on not long ago at age ninety-two, but Mary is still there on the ranch. She claims she won't leave unless they carry her out feet first. This shows the spirit of these great pioneers, who lived simply (not needing all the things we think necessary these days) and with total dedication to and love for the land.

I learned a lot about cattle from Joe, especially about interpreting tracks. Joe could tell you everything that went on out there just from looking at the tracks in the dirt. One day we were riding along, following some cattle, when Joe, looking down at the velvety red dust of the road, commented that Old Red had not yet dropped her calf. I asked how he knew it was Old Red. (Joe had names for every critter. To him, his cattle were as individual as people.) He told me that Old Red had caught her hoof in a barbed wire fence awhile back and had a notch in her left back hoof. When I asked how he knew she hadn't dropped her calf, his answer made sense. He pointed out the depth of hoofprints in the dust alongside the other cow prints, and sure enough, her prints were a half-inch deeper.

He also remarked that his neighbor had been to the

ranch during the afternoon. Again I asked how he could tell it was that neighbor, and Joe said the neighbor's old Ford had a distinctive tire tread. By paying attention to the road, Joe could tell what had gone on at the ranch all day.

One day when we were riding, he told us to bush up while he made a short run down a little side canyon. We sat there in the boiling sun, wondering what he meant by "bush up." Very soon the heat started to get to us, so we tied our horses under some big bushes and sat under a bush in what little shade there was. Belatedly it occurred to us that we were "bushed up."

I could go on and on about some of these old-timers and their stories, but I have other tales to tell. However, I will mention that Mary's mother and father were still living in Sedona then and had been here since 1909. A couple of times I had the good fortune to ride out with her father on short field trips, and he showed me some of the indigenous herbs and plants the early pioneers used. One was an herb that stopped bleeding; it was called devil's claw because the seed pod of the plant was shaped like a claw. When these claws would attach to the cattle's legs, the cattle would be frightened and start to run, sometimes causing a stampede. I remember that this plant had little reddish hairs just under the ground, attached to the roots. He told me they always kept a jar of it on hand for emergencies. If a little of this herb were packed into a cut or wound, the bleeding would stop immediately. I tried it, and it works.

I could tell more about these days, but that would require another book. I was truly blessed to know these wonderful pioneers and hear their stories and tales about early Sedona. These people were strong and self-reliant; they lived their lives with a sense of self-worth and freedom, which we no longer are able to experience as they did.

I hope Sedona's second round of pioneers, of which I am one, will also leave a proud legacy behind when we go.

Joe Hancock, Cattleman

My friend Joe Hancock had been a cattleman for years and years. He and his wife Mary had lived on their ranch in Loy Butte Canyon at least sixty-five years, and Mary is still there. Joe finally got to the place where he had to stand on a box to get on his horse. One day he said to me, "When you get to the place where you have to get on a box to mount your horse, it's time to quit." And he decided to give up most of his cattle and sell his cattle permit.

In those early days, cattlemen could get a cattle permit from the Forest Service. This permit allowed cattle owners to lease about one hundred acres of forest grazing land per head. For instance, if you owned fifty head of cattle, you could lease 5000 acres. Regardless of their owners, all the cattle ran loose on the leased land.

In the summer the cattle were taken to the top of the canyon where it was cooler and there was plenty of grass for grazing. The cowboys used to drive them up there on the old cattle trails. Later they went by truck.

In the fall all the calves were herded together and run through a cattle chute where the owners would claim their calves. The chute was near the **Hancock Ranch**, so at twelve o'clock all the cattlemen and cowboys would turn up at the Hancocks' for their noon dinner. Usually ten or twelve men would come, but Mary never knew just how many to cook for.

One time she was out of town for a couple of weeks, and I volunteered to do the cooking and serve dinner to the men. Mary had stocked her big ranch kitchen with huge roasts almost as large as the hindquarters of a cow, and lots of food. I did the best I could and somehow managed to cook the dinners.

After the men ate, they went outside to smoke and rest on the grass before going back to work. Meanwhile I washed the dishes, put them away and got into my riding breeches so I could help the men gather the cattle and drive them through the cattle chute.

One afternoon I was told to get into the chute to help push the calves through. One calf was exceptionally stubborn, and although I tried and tried, I couldn't push hard enough to budge it. "Twist its tail!" I was told. So I did. And that calf kicked me so hard in my solar plexus that he knocked me out. I was carried back to the ranch house, where I spent the rest of the day recuperating. Right then and there I made a solemn vow that never again would I get into a cattle chute.

Now, back to Joe's permit and his attempt to sell it. All sales transfers had to be approved by the Forest Service, and Joe couldn't to get any cooperation. What Joe had expected would be a simple transaction turned out to be an endless hassle of red tape. He thought the Forest Service was giving him a hard time and didn't know why.

Finally, a big cattle outfit with a herd of approximately 2000 head made Joe an offer that he considered to be ridiculously low. He suspected there must be some kind of collusion between that big outfit and the Forest Service, and he was really mad! He was so furious and frustrated that he decided to sell his cattle permit himself, but he had no success.

This is when he asked me if I would sell his permit. Now, I'd never attempted to sell a cattle permit, nor had I ever heard of anyone who had. I found out that the Forest Service recently had made a new rule: They would give out no more permits except to cattle ranchers who already had them.

When Sally came along, I thought we had a perfect buyer. She was an old-time cowgirl and cattle rancher who already had a cattle permit. Sally was a tough old gal who often rode with the men on her ranch and was accustomed to getting what she wanted. What she wanted now was to buy Joe's permit, and she made an offer, which Joe accepted. Then started months of delay and more red tape from the Forest Service. We made many trips to the Forest Service headquarters in Flagstaff and got nowhere. All of us were exasperated, especially Sally.

So one day Sally and I drove up to the headquarters and she took a tape recorder along with her. She slammed it down on the representative's desk and said, "Now, you SOB! You've been lying to me, and I'm tired of your lies! I'm recording every word you say from now on. Start talking!"

And do you know, from that moment on, the deal went through smoothly and quickly! I never could have sold Joe's cattle permit without Sally's help.

10

Red Hedges Buries Cisco

ed Hedges was one of Sedona's colorful characters and was much loved and cared for by the
locals. He slept in the wash on an old mattress under
the bridge on **Brewer Road**. One night during the monsoon season, a violent storm hit in the mountains above
us, but no rain fell in Sedona. We had no knowledge of
the storm until the middle of the night, when we were
awakened by a gigantic roar. A huge flash flood, seemingly out of nowhere, was rushing down the wash that
led into Oak Creek. Actually, the water overflowed the
road and came right up to our own front door.

The flood of angry water poured under the bridge
and carried Red and his old mattress along with it. Fortunately, Red was able to abandon his mattress in time
to avoid being dumped into the raging creek.

When the town's business people heard what had
happened, they were terribly concerned and set about
finding a safer and drier "bedroom" for Red. Someone

located an old shack where he could sleep without danger of flash floods, and someone else donated a dry mattress. Red was not at all happy about his new sleeping arrangement, insisting he'd much prefer to sleep under his bridge. His benefactors managed to persuade him to sleep in the little shack until the monsoons and possible flash floods were over. On Thanksgiving and Christmas I used to go to Red's shack with complete holiday dinners, and several other ladies also made a point of seeing that he always had food and other necessities.

Red was extremely proud of his army years in the service of his country, but unfortunately his addiction to wine had made his mind childlike and muddled. Sedona residents were aware of this, but accepted him as their lovable town drunk. A group of businessmen took it upon themselves to sort of look after him, providing him with shoes, shirts, socks, trousers and other articles of clothing when he seemed to be in need of them.

They also invented a job for him. He was to keep the sidewalk in front of the old Sedona Grocery Store and Pub clean and neat, and they gave him a big pushbroom to work with. Red was tremendously pleased with his job and felt very important. He was always out on the sidewalk, sweeping and tidying up after everyone. He would bow and tip his hat to the ladies like a proper gentleman and was regarded with real affection by Sedona's residents.

One time, a newcomer who wanted to do something important for Sedona decided that the old Hart irrigation ditch that ran along the left side of the street (now Highway 179) was wasting a lot of valuable water. "That water should be piped underground," he announced. And even though he did not own the property or the ditch, he set about installing pipes and filling in the ditch.

Along the side of the ditch grew several enormous old sycamore trees that were constantly watered by the ditch water, which was like a beautiful little creek running along under the trees The **Hideaway Restaurant** was built beside the ditch and had a broad deck with a railing.

From the dining tables on the deck one could look down on the ditch and watch the squirrels and birds that frequented the sycamores. The Hideaway became a favorite of the locals, who would gather there to eat, enjoy the view and feed the squirrels and birds all at the same time. It was truly delightful.

Now, when the water pipes were installed underground and the ditch filled, the magnificent old trees began to look like they were dying, and gradually the squirrels and birds began to disappear. This situation worried Red deeply and he complained about it often and loudly, but no one paid any attention. Finally he decided to take matters into his own hands.

At night he would sneak down to the ditch and punch holes in the water pipes so they would leak and water the suffering trees. Of course eventually Red was found out (by the man who had filled in the ditch) and was sternly reprimanded. Red was most unhappy when he had to quit punching his watering holes, but he was *really* upset when he saw a crew of men repairing the leaking pipes. I don't think all the leaks were found, because somehow the trees survived, although they never

Mary Lou and Glenn ride their horses in
Sedona's Saint Patrick's Day parade.

fully regained their former glory.

Glenn and I were genuinely fond of Red and enjoyed his free spirit and his childlike escapades. Little did we know what a role he was to play in our personal lives that involved one of our horses.

We really loved our horses. After we moved to Sedona, we made a special trip back to Oregon with a truck and horse trailer to bring Cisco and Poncho home with us. They were a beautiful pair of buckskins with black manes and tails. We often rode them in Sedona's Saint Patrick's Day parade and when we helped the Hancocks with their annual cattle roundup.

The old cowboys at that time didn't like to have a woman riding with them and did a lot of grumbling when I first showed up. But Joe Hancock told them I was just as good and capable a hand as they were, and eventually they grudgingly accepted me.

Cisco and Poncho took us on many an exploratory trip all around the Sedona area as well as up on the Frisco Peaks above Flagstaff. Those were wonderfully exciting and happy days.

Cisco was a remarkable horse who had several careers before we bought him. During WWII, when the California coastline was under constant vigilance, Cisco was there on daily patrol. One time Glenn and I rode our horses along the beachfront where Cisco had done his military duty, and Cisco was so delighted to be there that he acted like a young colt. He was also well-trained as a cutting horse, and for years had worked with range cattle. In spite of all his heavy duties he was gentle and well-behaved and had a winning personality.

Glenn Keller and Poncho.

Poncho was a people horse. Sociable and friendly. He had a mind of his own, and if I were riding out in the mountains he would often take me on a "shortcut" whether I wanted to or not. Usually I did not, for his shortcuts could be straight up a cliff, straight down, or both. When he was in this mood, I could depend on an exhilarating ride for sure.

At one point we had our horses pastured out behind our home, where Hillside Court now stands. At that time the Hollywood movie people were still filming up there and something was always going on. Cisco and Poncho made a habit of standing behind their fence, whinnying at the passersby. They became expert at begging for treats — apples and all kinds of goodies. In fact, with their charming ways, they became minor celebrities themselves.

Our horses were a major part of our lives, so you can imagine what a traumatic blow it was to us when our beautiful Cisco suddenly died out in the pasture on the 160-acre tract owned by our friend, Joe Hancock. Eventually this beautiful land was sold to a family who ran a popular dude ranch. It is called **El Rojo Grande Ranch**, and you can catch glimpses of it behind a white rail fence on Highway 89A about three miles out of town toward Cottonwood.

We wanted Cisco to be buried out there in that pasture. This would be quite an undertaking, because Cisco was a big horse, so Glenn asked Red he would take care of the burial. When Red wasn't busy polishing the sidewalk, he was available for odd jobs around Sedona, and he was glad to have the job.

So Glenn picked up Red in the morning and drove him out to the ranch along with the necessary tools for the job. He left Red to carry out his unhappy task. The day was warm, and as Glenn drove back to Sedona, he realized that Red would get mighty thirsty working out there in the sun. So he got a jug of water and drove back to the pasture. Red looked at the jug with unconcealed contempt and said, "I never touch it." Glenn went back to town and returned with a jug of wine, which suited Red just fine.

Personally, I doubted the wisdom of this and thought the jug of wine was a big mistake. However, everything seemed to go well because when Glenn returned later, he found Red waiting to be driven home, his mission accomplished.

I didn't go out right away to see where Cisco was buried because it was monsoon season and we'd had a big storm. A few days later after the storm had passed, Glenn and I drove out to the pasture to inspect the grave. Much to our horror, we found Cisco's legs — all four of them — sticking straight up out of the dirt. A shocking sight, as you can imagine.

Apparently Red had dug the grave and put our precious horse in it on his back, legs in the air. Since the grave was too shallow, he had covered Cisco's legs with a mound of loose dirt that had simply washed away in the heavy rainstorm. Not a dignified sight, but one that is indelibly imprinted in my memory. Much later we had many a laugh at this bizarre event, but at the time it was far from funny

Red Hedges is long since gone, but his personal story as well as the story about burying our horse are still capable of bringing a faint smile to my lips and a mist to my eye.

11

The Village of Oak Creek's Shady Past

annie was another tough old gal who graced Sedona from time to time. She was rumored to be a madam in Las Vegas, and I believe that rumor was true. She was especially intrigued by the area now known as the Village of Oak Creek and started to buy land there.

No one else was much interested in that property, which could be reached from Sedona by driving down a narrow, curving dirt road. If you took that road, you'd find nothing but vast acres of yucca, which in those days were called the Lord's candles. It is true that the expanse of endless meadows was a beautiful sight, and the scenery was gorgeous. But what use could the land be without water? So Fanny didn't have any competition.

She would come to Sedona and buy up land down there, approximately forty acres at a time, for which she paid almost nothing. Over the years she kept coming back and buying more parcels of land, until she finally owned about 2000 acres.

Then the amazing Fannie went to the expense of having three wells drilled in different places on her property to prove that water was available. All three wells were good and there was plenty of water.

One day Fannie came into my real estate office and said she wanted to sell all her acreage. She wanted one million dollars in cash. She would accept no payment unless the buyer delivered the million into her hot little hands, and this transaction was to take place only in Mexico.

I was rapidly learning not to be surprised at any-thing — not even this unusual demand. So I made out a listing, went to the courthouse and looked up all her parcels of land. Then I drew a large map that showed her properties and how they were situated in relation to one another. Most of it was adjoining, but not all of it.

Before long Fannie stopped in my office and I showed her the map. She was delighted! She snatched it off my desk and started out the door. I said, "Wait a minute. That's *my* map!" and she said, "The hell it is! It's *my* land and it's *my* map." And off she went. I had to do the job all over again so I could show it to prospective buyers.

The sad ending of this story is that Fannie never found a buyer, and she passed on before she could enjoy the fruits of her labors. She left all the land to an older sister who was in her nineties and living in a rest home. Soon the sister also passed on, and I don't know who in-herited Fannie's estate. But I do know that several years later the land was sold.

The original developers of Fannie's acreage divided it

into residential lots and started to sell them by mail. They advertised by sending out beautiful brochures showing the fabulous scenic area along with a map of the lots. Unsuspecting buyers were taken in by the promotion and had no idea that there were no streets (the map showed streets), no electricity, no telephones, no water — in fact, there were no improvements at all. The land just rested there peacefully in its virgin beauty, all meadows and yucca plants. Another deceit was in the name the developers gave to their project. They called it the Village of Oak Creek, and in truth, the creek was not even near the lots.

In no time the entire "development" was in the courts as disappointed buyers sued and sued. The entire situation was an embarrassment to the State of Arizona. This notoriety was not exactly the type of publicity Arizona welcomed. As for me, I just pretended that area didn't exist, and I *never* sold any land out there.

For about ten years the project didn't go anywhere because everything was held up in litigation. Finally, some of the original buyers got together and formed an association to handle the mess.

Now those acres of yucca and meadow have been replaced by beautiful houses and condominiums, flourishing businesses, hotels, shops and golf courses. Tourists as well as residents delight in the magnificent grandeur of **Bell Rock** and **Courthouse Rock**, both famous red rock landmarks. Indeed, the Village of Oak Creek is a thriving community with a population of approximately 6000 and growing.

Now you know the fascinating history of how the Village of Oak Creek came to be — a true story very few people know. Wouldn't Fannie be amazed!

12

Abe Miller and Tlaquepaque

The Abe Miller story is one that should be told, so here it is. Back in the sixties and seventies, Abe and I knew each other through our work, he as a Sedona builder and I as a real estate broker. At that time he was interested in buying three acres of land beside Oak Creek, a mile or so past the "Y" intersection on Highway 179 where the bridge goes over Oak Creek.

Whenever we would run into each other, he would say, "Let's have a cup of coffee." So we'd go into the **Ranch Kitchen** and have our coffee. (The Ranch Kitchen today is still in the same location and has the same name.) While we drank coffee, at some point he would ask, "Do you really think that guy who owns those three acres will sell? Because if he does, I'd like to make him an offer."

"I'm sure he'll sell if he gets the right offer," I'd say. And Abe would write an offer on his paper napkin and I'd take it to Mr. Girard, the owner of the land.

Girard would say, "No, I won't do this and I won't do that," as he checked off items, wrote his counteroffer on the napkin and handed it back to me. So back I'd go to Abe, paper napkin in hand. Abe would decide that Mr. Girard really didn't want to sell the three acres after all and we'd best forget it.

About a month later we'd meet on the street and he'd say, "Let's have a cup of coffee," and we'd go to the Ranch Kitchen and repeat the whole process. "Do you really think that guy will sell that property? If so, I'd like to make him an offer." And he'd write his offer on his paper napkin and away I'd go to see Mr. Girard. He'd turn it down and back I'd go to Abe with the paper napkin counteroffer. At one point, the waitress accidently threw the paper napkin away. After a frenzied search, it was dug out of the trash bin.

Abe and I and Mr. Girard went through this rigamarole for six months, and I sort of gave up on the whole thing. Then one day I said to myself, "I know that in the real estate business it's a no-no to bring the buyer and the seller together when negotiating, but what do I have to lose?" So I took Abe to meet Mr. Girard, and they hit it off on the spot. I just sat there doing nothing and watched them put the deal together. Abe took it home, wrote it up, and that was that.

These two men agreed to leave every tree standing where it was on the property, except for those in the way of a building or street. (And this was long before we became aware of tree conservation.) Abe held to this agreement, even to the point of building around the existing trees.

Before Abe started work on his building, he built a solid wall all along the highway at the edge of the property. This piqued everyone's curiosity. Even the **Red**

Rock News was upset because Abe wouldn't tell what he was going to build behind that wall. When asked, he just said, "You'll find out when I get it finished." This was even more annoying — after all, in a village as small as Sedona, doesn't everybody know everything that goes on?

Abe Miller's dream was to build a beautiful complex of shops where artwork and crafts would be created and sold by the artists who would live in quarters above the shops, as they often did in Mexico. Although this arrangement didn't work out, the buildings were built according to plan.

But first he flew his architects and working crew down to the Mexican town of Tlaquepaque, about three miles out of Guadalajara, to observe the buildings and learn how they were built. He brought back artifacts to use such as Mexican tile, art objects and oxen yokes, which he made into chandeliers. He gave me one of the yokes, and I have it over my rose arbor. He did everything he could to make his buildings as authentic as possible.

After his creation was completed, Abe just couldn't stay away from it. He worked around the grounds doing maintenance work and caring for the gardens. When someone would ask him, "Where can I find Mr. Miller?" he would say, "Oh, he's always around here someplace." He seemed to enjoy his little joke. One day a tourist remarked to Abe, "What a shame they've taken this marvelous old monastery and turned it into a shopping center." Abe told me later, "That was the best compliment I ever got."

Abe Miller gave Sedona one of the most beautiful shopping centers in the world. It's name, of course, is Tlaquepaque. Tlaquepaque is loved by Sedonans as

well as visitors and is one of Sedona's most famous tourist attractions.

13

Vortexes and the Ruby Focus

*A*mong metaphysical students, Sedona has long been known as a spiritual place that attracts many people in search of spiritual understanding. Because I arrived in Sedona over forty years ago, I can tell you the story of Sedona's early metaphysical beginnings. When I moved here in March 1957, I felt that this red rock country was my long-lost home, and that feeling is still with me. Never have I had a desire to leave in all this time.

During those years I have read countless books and articles and listened to many lectures and tapes about Sedona's vortexes — many of these offered by newcomers who claimed to have discovered them. So perhaps now is the time to tell the true story about their discovery.

Some people claim that all of Sedona is a vortex, a power place of spiraling energy turning either clockwise or counterclockwise. Many claims have been made about meditations, healings, visions, sightings and channelings of a psychic nature and other unusual experiences due to vortex energies. These tales of otherworldly happenings are in no way new discoveries by contemporary man. Far from it.

We must go back several thousand years to find the first people, the Native Americans, who knew about the vortex energies in this area and came here for healing and spiritual experiences. They called Sedona the Land of Fire.

Then about thirty-five years ago a small group who called themselves the **Ruby Focus** arrived in Sedona from Phoenix, saying that St. Germain had directed them to start a center here. They came to my real estate office (a glassed-in front porch of my large home on Highway 179 where I lived, had my church and carried on my business) and told me a story about channeled information describing an exact location near a vortex, where there would be a four-bedroom house and some acreage suitable for their center. From their description I knew immediately the place they seemed to be describing. (In those days there were very few homes that large available.) I took them to see the property, a three-acre ranch at the foot of **Airport Hill**, on which there were two four-bedroom houses separated by several acres. The Ruby Focus group got all excited after seeing one of the houses, saying they thought this was the place they had been directed to.

When we returned to my office, they asked if I had a large, round table where they could channel. I took them into my kitchen and got them settled around the table. I was sneaking out quietly when they called me back and insisted I had to be a part of the channeling. Evangeline and Carmen VanPollen headed this group,

Evangeline being the main channel.

To my amazement, Evangeline was given an enthusiastic go-ahead by St. Germain, Sananda and others, who commented that the house they were to purchase was located very close to the property I had shown them. However, the house that would be right for them was near the strongest vortex in the area between two hills and on the way to the airport, called **Saddlerock**. With this information, I realized they were being directed to the second house on the ranch. So I took them there, and when the group saw this place, they knew it was where they were to be.

Two weeks later several of them came back, bringing their cots and food, all prepared to settle down in my living room. They just took my place over for the weekend, visiting the property and then making their offer.

The group had only $1000 for earnest money, but they were instructed to open the transaction with that amount and to agree to $4000 more in thirty days, then go into a ninety-day escrow, at which time (they had been told) they would have the balance of the money. I was astounded when the owners of the home accepted the offer. This was the most fantastic test of faith I had ever witnessed, but the next four months proved their faith well-founded, for the money came in miraculously right on target.

The group came up from Phoenix every few weeks to sit up there in the vortex, insisting that I go along and be a part of it. We were directed to do certain chants and affirmations while sending the energy of the vortex to their future property just below. I have to admit I was more than embarrassed sitting out there on the hill chanting, hoping all the time that no one would see me. It was pretty "far out" in those days for a real estate person to be acting this way. I had already suffered much criticism from the orthodox community for teaching hatha yoga — and now *this!*

The elderly couple who started the group had many happy and successful years with their center before they passed on, Evangeline at the age of eighty-seven and Carmen at ninety-one. The reins were handed to others in the group, who changed the name to **Rainbow Focus** and are still there doing their work.

I am proud to say that I had a part in this wonderful example of faith. The Ruby Focus group was given knowledge of the vortexes long before anyone else discovered them, except for the ancient Native Americans.

Over the years I have observed that few people can live close to a vortex for very long. In the Saddlerock subdivision just below the vortex, a year is about average, so there is a lot of real estate activity in that area. I personally lived with a small vortex in my back yard for seventeen years, and every psychic who came to my place pinpointed the exact location. One even buried a crystal in the center of it. Clairvoyants observed that elves, fairies and devas carefully avoided that spot. I kept quiet about it, though — I wanted no hordes tramping through my quiet hideaway. There are more vortexes than *anyone* knows about in this sacred red rock paradise. And there are a lot of mysteries here yet to be solved.

14

First Meditation Group

id you know that about thirty-five years ago, when Sedona's population had grown to about 3500 residents, a meditation group met together every week or so in Sedona? Well, it did, and we made it a gala event. Back in those days there wasn't much to do in the evening unless someone generated a get-together of some kind.

We held our meditation at Millie Sampson's house because she had a big green lawn where we could spread out our potluck supper, and afterward we held our meditation and discussion. This group did not smoke or drink, and our potluck before the meditation was a form of social activity, which gave us a lot of pleasure. Happily, it was not involved with the usual "fors" and "againsts" that often occur in many group gatherings.

Our meditation leader was a psychic who drove down from Flagstaff every week with his wife and another couple who had been disciples of Paramahansa

Yogananda. Altogether our numbers varied from twelve to twenty. This leader regularly admonished us for reading too much and kept insisting that we stop giving ourselves "mental indigestion." "You have reached saturation," he would say. All went well until a new person joined our group, a take-charge kind of person who suggested just the opposite, listing several books we should be reading.

This started a lot of hassling between the two, and soon we stopped meeting because we found ourselves taking sides. Stormy discussions and arguments weren't what we wanted.

When our group broke up, Lois Binford, who was one of our members (now Mrs. Bob Proctor), started her own group. This group met every week for years, helping lost souls find and advance into Light. This important rescue work is being carried on by dedicated workers all over the world. Their purpose is to help free Earthbound souls so they may progress in spirit. Those who do this work must have a deep love for all people, a pure desire to help and have a thorough understanding of the problem.

Meanwhile, many in our original group really missed getting together and later decided to meet for potluck and music so we could dance. This became great fun (with no disputes), and when this group grew to over twenty, we had to rent a larger space for dancing. Sometimes we rented the clubhouse at **Sedona Shadows**, and that building is still there. Other times we rented the clubhouse at **Sunset Mobile Park**. Someone would bring a stereo and records; we had a lovely time dancing. It was a great way to get acquainted, good recreation, splendid exercise and a fun way to spend an evening.

There were always more women than men at these

events, so we began to dance separately. Even the men danced alone now and then, and each one danced to his/her own interpretation of the music and rhythm as he/she felt it. We called ourselves the Happy Nuts, because if a stranger had happened to look in while we were dancing, he would have thought it a bit weird to see a roomful of people dancing alone. In those days people did not dance in public without a partner as they do now.

One time we decided to come dressed as what we thought we'd been in a past life. I remember going as a ballerina in a tutu and ballet slippers. It was amazing what that costume did for me. I went leaping and whirling around the room on cloud nine. Up to that time I had been pretty prim and proper. At first, every time I got up to dance alone, I felt like a fool and quickly sat down. I really had a hard time with that. I was painfully stiff and self-conscious, but finally I got with it and loosened up. When my friends began to call me Mary Lou, the Rag Doll, I considered it a real compliment.

Actually, we got more benefit from this phase than we did with our meditation group because we learned to express freedom and joy in movement. Interestingly, no one drank beforehand, and those who wanted to smoke went outside. We were having such a lively and fun time, apparently liquor and cigarettes were not needed.

Much has been lost in social relationships with the advent of TV, VCRs and other mind-grabbers. This was a refreshing and innocent time in the history of Sedona, and it will live long in our memories. A few of those involved are still here, and when we run into each other now and then, we reminisce and declare, "Those certainly *were* the good old days."

15

First Yoga Class

*A*bout thirty-five years ago I was teaching hatha yoga in Sedona. At that time yoga was little known and certainly was misunderstood by the local orthodox community. I was often criticized and maligned for my efforts, some people even branding me evil. Many a nose was elevated and many a head turned away when I appeared in public. Of course I felt terrible about this, but nevertheless I went right on teaching. I often heard a class member say irritably, "Why do you have to give us that spiritual stuff? I came here for exercise." I tried to explain that hatha yoga means "union with God," and that its purpose is to learn the mental, physical and spiritual disciplines that make this union possible.

Needless to say, I lost a lot of students who came only for the physical exercise. I would start class with twenty to thirty pupils, and gradually some would drop out until there would be only six to eight left. These few really came to learn, which made it seem a worthwhile effort.

One evening two long-haired teenage boys arrived unexpectedly and asked if they could join the class. I could see no reason why not, so I gave my consent. They went into the restroom and came out dressed in karate attire and placed their mats on the floor, looking eager to begin. To my consternation, at least half of the ladies immediately picked up their mats and towels and moved to the other side of the room. I couldn't believe it! I had been teaching, among other things, oneness, tolerance and understanding of one's fellow man, so I was amazed at this display of separativeness. The boys were clean and polite and showed unusual knowledge of hatha yoga, so I could not understand why half of my class so obviously rejected our visitors.

When I returned home that evening, I received several irate phone calls from some of my students, demanding to know if those hippie boys would be coming back. Now, I had never seen these young men before and had no way of knowing if they would return. I pointed out that the boys were clean, polite, well-behaved and knowledgeable students. I refused to agree that I'd turn them away if they did come again, and I asked what they had done to annoy the ladies so. The answer was, "But they are long-haired hippies, and I do not want to be associated with them." Wasn't that just dandy!

I mentioned that the boys had the right to wear their hair in any fashion they wished and that they were some mothers' sons. Nothing I had to say seemed to have the slightest effect on my students' disapproval. I felt that my seven years as a yoga teacher had been wasted if my class could be this discriminatory over long hair.

Shortly after that I gave up teaching yoga and decided that those boys dropped in just to help me see a truth I had not been aware of, that I was wasting my time. I never saw them again.

During the years I taught yoga, I can remember several serious students who stuck with it and made progress. So looking back, I see that my efforts were not wasted entirely, and I myself learned a lot about human nature.

I have been pleased that now others are teaching hatha yoga in Sedona, and I sincerely hope that the experience will prove meaningful, not only to the students but also to the teachers, as it was to me. I believe that at this time and place, people are more open-minded and tolerant. Perhaps they are far more ready for the wonderful experience of the teaching and can embrace *all* that this discipline offers — the mental and spiritual benefits as well as the physical.

And yes, I still do a few minutes of hatha yoga every morning. A few gentle yoga stretches do wonders for my old bones and peace of mind.

16

Beating Out Anger
at a Love-in

From the early years of Sedona's metaphysical community, I have resurrected an almost forgotten experience of about thirty-eight years ago. A friend, who had at one time been a deputy sheriff in Sedona but was now living in Flagstaff, was a very troubled man. He had some deep emotional scars that dated way back to childhood. This man not only had had an alcoholic father who had been very abusive, but he had spent most of his adult life as a deputy sheriff, a forest ranger and in other aspects of law enforcement, which was a life that focused almost entirely on crime and violence.

He had heard about a weekend retreat up on the Zuni reservation; I believe the small town was called Azteca. The retreat was geared to help people get rid of old emotional scars and hatreds. My friend wanted very much to attend, but hesitated to go alone. He offered to pay my way if I would accompany him. I was not at all enthused about going, but he was desperate to try something that might help him get rid of his violent moods, so I finally agreed to go.

The group at the retreat was a large one, and we gathered in a big building that was to be our place of destiny for two days. There were couples who were angry with each other, on the verge of divorce; a mother and father with a son who were warring; a mother and daughter who were trying to come to terms with each other; and many others who needed emotional healing.

Each of us was taken into a small cell-like room with both a female and a male counselor. The room was equipped with a stuffed and padded object and we were given a short length of hose. I was told to get rid of my deep hatred and anger by beating on the object with the hose. I kept insisting I had no hate or anger left after many years of working my way through those things. This seemed to really anger my counselors.

They called me a liar and said I was not being honest with myself, that surely I must have some hatred toward my father. I tried to explain that many years ago I did have some resentment toward my father, but since his death I had come to terms with my feelings and released the emotion. They refused to believe this and insisted that I beat out my anger toward my father. Even though I felt this was ancient history, I halfheartedly beat the padded object in order to placate them. I finally gave up, but I heard loud banging noises coming from the other rooms. l was told that those people were being honest with themselves and coming to terms with their problems.

In complete disgust, they finally dismissed me, and I

left the little room feeling that somehow I had been a total failure. Later my friend told me the exercise had done him a great deal of good. Crying and sobbing, he had gone into a frenzy of beating his father. He felt that he had rid himself of an enormous burden. This beating exercise must have been appropriate, because later in the day, as the group began to emerge and gather together, I could see that the participants were more relaxed and no longer angry. Lots of tears and hugs were being openly displayed. We spent the rest of the retreat in workshops and lectures on self-love and forgiveness.

Because we were spending hours of sitting, which was tiresome, we were given a break from time to time so we could get up and stretch. I was asked to lead the group through some simple stand-up exercises. I was a hatha yoga teacher in those days, hence the request for my assistance, and I was pleased to help.

On the last day we all hiked up a wooded canyon and up the side of a mountain to a large cave, where a loudspeaker had been set up and a man with a wonderful voice presented the Sermon on the Mount. It was a very moving experience, beautifully done with low background music. I felt it was the highlight of the retreat.

Later on that last evening we all gathered to participate in a ceremony much like a graduation. We were asked to come forward and express our feelings and comments about what had occurred during the seminar. In addition, we were encouraged to share any bad feelings or resentments we might have toward anyone in the group and try to get rid of our negativity.

One young woman, who was quite overweight and dowdy, got up to speak and said, "I hate you, yoga teacher." I gasped in amazement, wondering what I could have said or done to offend her. When I asked her why, she said she hated me because I was slender and was everything she thought she was not. I talked to her about it and tried to convince her that if she really wanted to improve her looks, she could do it with determination and perseverance. I told her that it was not easy for me to maintain my figure and energy, and that I had to work at it. Finally, with a tearful hug, she "forgave" me.

Many grievances were aired and forgiven that evening. A young man stood up and said, "I hate you too, yoga teacher." Again I asked why. He said he was very familiar with hatha yoga and I was just like all the rest of the Western yoga teachers. I was doing only the exercise part and completely ignoring the spiritual aspect.

I had to remind him publicly that a yogi did only what he was asked to do, that I would have been infringing on the purpose of the retreat leaders if I had opted to do more than I was asked to do. I also told him that I did indeed teach the spiritual aspect of yoga. He understood what I was saying and came to me with a big hug. I was absolutely amazed at how quickly and innocently I had made enemies.

I learned so much by just being an observer of this process. Looking back on the experience, I can see that a lot of emotional healing actually took place over that weekend. It was a real love-in.

17

First Unity Church

So many things have happened in Sedona over the years I have lived here, I could never run out of stories of the many exciting and wonderful events that were the beginning of our present metaphysical community. It occurred to me that readers might like to know how the first **Unity Church** came to be in Sedona. Of course I realize that if one person had not done it, another eventually would have, but it was a dynamic and interesting man who came with the dream and the energy to make it happen when it did.

For some strange reason, I always became involved in these happenings, and somehow the old Keller Building (which has now gone on to whatever heaven old buildings go to) was usually where all these things took place. I did not plan it that way, spirit just sort of took over and although I did not always understand it, I was able to "go with the flow," as the New Age generation puts it. I don't take any credit for whatever happened, because something else was doing it. All I did was carry the ball, so to speak.

Dale Batesole, a Unity minister and teacher, lived in Scottsdale but was constantly being drawn to Sedona. He started a class here in a private home teaching a type of psycho-cybernetics. I joined his class and learned many things, not only from his teaching but also from knowing this charismatic man.

At that time I was a part of the **Crescent Moon Ranch** group studying Sri Aurobindo's writings. Dale attended also and made the comment that it was the type of group he would love to be a part of, but he felt the Unity teaching was more suited to the general public, which was just beginning to open to New Age teachings. He thought he could do more good with Unity as his teaching tool, and his dream was to start a Unity church in Sedona. He was a highly developed spiritual being who seemed to know what his role was in getting across the message of the Aquarian Age, and he was single-focused in his drive to fulfill his destiny as he saw it.

Unfortunately, the head church in Phoenix did not share Dale's dream; they instructed him to start a Unity church in Flagstaff, not Sedona. They felt that Sedona was far too small and not ready for it. So Dale rented a place in Flagstaff and began his ministry, but few people came to hear him speak. Each Sunday he noted with interest that five or six people drove all the way from Sedona to be a part of his small congregation. He kept telling the heads of the church in Phoenix that more Sedona people were interested than Flagstaff people, but they would not give in, and refused to help him financially to start a church in Sedona.

I will never forget the day he came to my real estate office and asked me to help him find a place to rent for a church. Here he could try out his theory that Sedona was a far more fertile location for the church, but he would have to rely on his own funds to show the hierarchy he was right. It was one of those unusual gray rainy days, so rare in Sedona, and we dashed in and out of the rain looking at several possibilities. Somehow none of them would do, either because they were not large enough or the rent was more than he could afford.

We came back to my office and were discussing the situation in the big room, which had become a focal point for many metaphysical and psychic happenings. In those days there were very few halls or places where a group meeting could be held. (Now there are many choices.) I could see that his determination had become almost an obsession. He *must* start a Unity church in Sedona no matter what obstacles were in his way.

Suddenly, without even thinking about it, I blurted out an offer to let him use my building without charge so that he could prove what he felt so strongly. It was my attempt to help and to show him I had confidence in him. He was so overwhelmingly delighted that he strode around the room figuring how many chairs he could get in and where the organ would be placed. In the years that followed he never let me forget that my decision that day to lend my building was the impetus that made the Unity Church become a reality in Sedona.

In three months he often had as many as fifty people in his congregation, and there were wall-to-wall chairs, with some people sitting on the floor. This was just about full capacity for the space. In six months he had sixty people coming regularly, and the elders of the Phoenix church came up to witness what he had done in such a short time. They could hardly believe it, but as a consequence they helped him rent a building on 89A at the base of Airport Road, later occupied by the Hathaway Shirt Company and now by Crimson Cliffs and Raven's Nest.

Within a year he had as many as eighty-five in his congregation, and the building became too small. This prompted the mother church to help him buy the building that is the present Unity Church on Deer Trail Drive. He was a great teacher, an inspired minister and attracted a large following. Yes, Dale Batesole was right: Sedona *was* ready for a Unity church.

After a few years he was offered a much larger church in Palm Springs, California, and he decided to accept it. The little church in Sedona suffered greatly from his absence, and several ministers have come and gone. I understand that the present minister is an old friend of Dale's and that the church is doing well. But soon after Dale left, the congregation dropped to half its former size. It seemed it was Dale Batesole who made it happen, and without him many lost interest. Eventually he started a TV ministry that became very successful. It has reached thousands, maybe by this time millions. He was one of the many unusual and gifted people who came into early Sedona to assist it in becoming a center of New Age teaching.

18

Flagstaff

Have you heard that our sister city, Flagstaff, is probably the most integrated city in the United States? In the early days there were some huge sawmills in Flagstaff, and timber was being cut in every direction. They left the large trees in Oak Creek Canyon and up on the peaks where the Snow Bowl is, thank goodness, but the rest was laid bare with nothing left but stumps.

Zane Grey wrote *Call of the Canyon* about that time, and he lamented at great length about the devastation of thousands of acres of ponderosa pine. The forest you now see is second growth. Zane Grey's book was about Oak Creek Canyon and West Fork, and his description of the area as it was then was beautiful. If you have never read it, you have a treat in store.

Also about that time the railroad was coming across the country from the East, and Flagstaff began to come alive. Blacks, Chinese and Mexicans were brought in to work in the lumber industry and the oncoming railroad. There were Whites and Native Americans also in the grand mixture, and these races grew up together. I think they are in the third generation now. Interracial marriages further integrated the melting pot. Having grown up together, they all seemed to accept each other without too much conflict, and in time (except for some newcomers) the community of Flagstaff accepted each other and learned to live, work and go to school together with no one paying much attention to the color of skin. Somehow they have gotten along pretty peacefully all these years while the rest of the nation was torn with racial strife.

At one time, about thirty-five years ago, I remember hearing over the radio that a busload of militant Blacks were coming across old 66, which was considered the main street of America at that time because it went from the East Coast to the West Coast. These Blacks were stirring up trouble in every city and town as they came, but when they arrived in Flagstaff they were greeted by a group of Flagstaff's Black community, who refused to let them get off the bus. They were told that they did not have any trouble there and certainly did not want any trouble. They told the group in the bus to drive on down the road and dump their trouble somewhere else.

At the time I thought it was such a great story that someone would surely print it. As far as I know, no one did write it, so now I feel it is time to speak up and tell the story about one city in America where everyone accepts everyone else with no fanfare, no big deal, just a live-and-let-live way of life. No one forced them to live together and get along with each other; it just happened naturally over the years.

74

This was a melting pot that just melted together with no one paying much attention to what was happening. Isn't that the way it should be?

19

Curse of the Medicine Man

On the late seventies a group of us, including a couple of gurus, decided to try to break the "curse" that, as rumor had it, had been put on the building presently known as the **Enchantment Resort.**

The original builders, a couple from Wyoming, had purchased (from whom, I don't know) about sixty-five acres in this spectacular area and built an enormous house. After the death of his wife, the owner could not bear to stay there, so he sold the property. Then began a series of new owners who used the house as a lodge, a hotel, a resort and so on, and in due time every one of them went broke.

The gossip around Sedona was that the original builder had paved over an old Native American burial ground, thus provoking the ill-will of a powerful medicine man. So it came to pass that anyone who built on that sacred land was doomed to bad luck and financial disaster. How much of this story is true, I cannot say, but I do know that the property has lost money at least three times.

Several of us had heard the story and observed the beautiful land of Enchantment struggling time and time again under financial distress. We were taken up with the idea of doing our metaphysical thing and removing the curse on the land.

So, with the very best of intentions, we made our plans and met out there one afternoon. We formed a circle, held hands, addressed the spirits of the area, asked forgiveness for desecrating the holy land and prayed that the curse be lifted. We went through some cleansing rituals and ceremonies and walked around the property. Then we went into silent meditation and reverie.

When we had done all we could and were regrouping to leave, we discovered that one of the girls in our group was missing. We called and looked everywhere for her, to no avail. She seemed to have vanished into thin air. People were getting a bit nervous, wondering what could have happened, when suddenly here she came, stumbling out of the brush looking terribly distraught.

"I went into deep meditation," she gasped, "and found myself way back in time. I was the medicine man who cursed this place!" And she broke down as she told us of her pain and distress.

I found her experience especially meaningful when she mentioned that the medicine man had spent his lifetime working with healing herbs for his tribe and was considered very special. I happened to know that this girl was exceptionally interested in native herbs, for many a time I had shown her land suitable for the herb farm she dreamed of starting in Sedona someday.

After she had settled down a bit, we got in the cars to

leave, only to find that all the employees had left and locked the gate behind them. We couldn't drive out.

While a heated discussion went on about the possibility of spending the night right there, I went over to look at the gate. After all, I'd been a farm girl and knew gates pretty well. It didn't take long for me to figure out what to do. I simply took the hinges off the gate, the cars drove through and the gate was replaced.

To this day I don't know if our serious efforts did any good, but I sincerely hope the present owners of the beautiful Enchantment Resort do well financially and in all ways.

PART TWO

Leaders and Followers

20

Three Visionaries

Manley P. Hall, Philosopher . . .

Manley P. Hall, one of the greatest philosophers of our time, made his transition on August 29, 1990, at the age of eighty-nine. This event brought back memories of about forty years ago. A friend had given me a tape of a Manley P. Hall lecture and said he would mail me one every week if I could find a few people interested enough to come and listen to it. I decided to give it a try and put a small notice in the *Red Rock News* announcing that there would be a free taped lecture.

Much to my surprise, a dozen or more people showed up. I had an old Roberts reel-to-reel recorder to play it on (we didn't have cassette tapes back then). The lecture was so well accepted and appreciated that I decided to present one on a weekly basis. Sometimes twenty or more people would show up, and I had to keep providing more chairs or pillows to sit on. This was the very beginning of a semblance of a metaphysical group in Sedona proper. There had been a regular meeting at the Crescent Moon (Duncan) Ranch for many years before that, but it was well out of town and did not attract the tourists and those drifting in and out of Sedona.

Manley's lectures were really wonderful, and many came to hear them over the next few years. The one I liked best was titled "Who Is Tampering with the Soul of America?" Of course everyone was sure he was going to say the Communists, but to our surprise we found the culprits to be ourselves! Through lack of interest and apathy we were accepting everything that was handed to us through the news media, churches and governments. He suggested that physically, mentally and spiritually we were becoming a zombie nation and were gradually deteriorating. Many years later we can see how right he was. I still have that tape and consider it one of my prize possessions.

I remember that he urged the mothers and wives of America to start becoming aware of this problem, for they alone could change the course of history by making their families aware of what was happening. He advised us to go through the grocery store reading labels before we bought our food, for even back then we were being poisoned at our food source.

After I put on my glasses to read the fine print on labels, I was horrified to see what I had been eating. I began to tell the grocery store owner that if he would get pure food, I would be able to buy more groceries. I got groups of women together to encourage them to read labels, but I met very little interest. Most bought what had the most colorful and interesting labels or was advertised on the radio. (We didn't have television in Sedona in those days.) Now we are constantly bombarded with TV commercials that influence our eating habits to an alarming degree

In May 1987 we were blessed with Manley P. Hall's actual physical presence, thanks to the **Beacon Light Center**, which had arranged his four-day visit in Sedona. He was a 33rd-degree Mason and was given a wonderful reception at the **Masonic Hall**, which was filled to overflowing that night.

Manley also gave a lecture at the Flicker Shack to a full house; some people couldn't get in and were turned away. His health at that time was precarious, and he had to be helped to a chair on the stage. But in spite of his frailty, I have never heard a speaker who was able to speak for three hours without boring anyone, without missing a word or stumbling over a phrase. He never made a mistake.

In sixty years he gave 7500 lectures in the United States and abroad, and his books have been published in many foreign languages. This remarkable man was asked to speak at the Smithsonian Institution and Harvard on alchemy, a subject he had written about in great depth. It has been reported that Manley P. Hall had one of the six highest IQs known to man.

In recent years, because of his failing health, he had not been out of Los Angeles to speak except for his last appearance in Sedona in 1987. He loved this area and vowed he would return, but his time ran out before he was able to make that dream come true. While he was here a group of musicians from Flagstaff gave a concert, playing music inspired by St. Germain. This was the first time this music had been played in 250 years, and it was played especially in Manley's honor. The Beacon Light Center gave him a small reception, but he was unable to walk into the house. He was very ill and sat out in the car in the driveway. We all took turns going out to visit with him. I had a chance to tell him that his taped lectures were responsible for getting the whole metaphysical movement going in Sedona.

Manley P. Hall has left us with another precious memory, as he was one of the great ones who came to Sedona over the last forty years to shed his light in our time.

Ralph, Mary Lou and friend with her turquoise jeep.

Ralph Bergstresser and Nicola Tesla, Inventors . . .

One of the most interesting friends I made in my Sedona sojourn was Ralph Bergstresser. At the time I met him about thirty-eight years ago, he lived in Hollywood, California. He was deeply involved then (and still is) in manufacturing his Purple Energy Plates and other inventions, which he attributed to the genius scientist, Nikola Tesla. In Ralph's youth he knew Tesla and often spent time with him, fascinated by his research and many wonderful inventions. Tesla was investigating in areas far ahead of his time, but Ralph had a scientific mind and could understand the work his friend was doing.

Ralph has told me that Tesla was a very lonely man who was not appreciated by his contemporaries because he was so advanced in his thinking and work. Very few minds back then were ready for what he was interested in: the alternating-current generator; a system for long-distance electrical transmission; the wireless broadcasting of electricity through the air; the Tesla coil, widely used now in radio and television; remote control and on and on.

After Tesla's death in 1943, Ralph became one of the first to make practical use of some of his friend's ideas. One of Ralph's best-known inventions is his Purple Energy Plate, inspired by Tesla's theories. These plates come in two sizes, 2¼" by 4½" and 12" by 12". They are made of anodized aluminum, in which the atomic structure has been altered so they resonate with the basic energy of the universe. They are not charged; they use *free universal energy*. They create an energy field around themselves, and by osmosis the energy can penetrate any living thing. This energy is beneficial to all life — plant, animal and human.

Ralph describes this Purple Plate energy as positive energy, or God power, and reminds us that love is positive energy: God is love, God is energy. Scientific studies have proven that by projecting love to a plant, it will flourish and grow more vigorously than a similar plant that has not received the positive energy of love. In India this life-force energy is called prana and in China it is known as chi.

Ralph's Purple Plates, Green Thumb Energy Tubes and other related inventions are sold all over the world. His representatives sell his products in South America,

China, Holland, Germany, the Netherlands, as well as in Canada, the United States and other countries. Often these people would come to visit Ralph in Scottsdale. He was always generous with his fascinating friends and would bring them to Sedona to meet me. I would act as the tour guide and show them all around the Sedona I love so much.

I always looked forward to Ralph's frequent visits. He and his interesting, stimulating friends really spiced up my life. He and I were never romantically involved, but ours is an unusually close relationship that means a lot to me.

Ralph Bergstresser and Mary Lou on top of Doe Mountain.

At one point I sold him a house in Sedona, in my neighborhood. He enjoyed playing host to his many friends, and when special guests were here from out of state or other countries, we often went to **Shugrue's Restaurant** for dinner together. Eventually, the long drive to and from Scottsdale became overly tiring for him. He had me sell his house, and he moved back to Scottsdale where his manufacturing plant is located. We still keep in touch by telephone.

Cleve Backster, Scientist . . .

Among the many fascinating people who have come through Sedona in the past is Cleve Backster, the man who did the research for the book *The Secret Life of Plants*. He was one of the many special people that Ralph Bergstresser, my dear friend of some thirty-eight years, brought to Sedona to meet me. It has been through Ralph's generous habit of sharing his famous friends that I have met so many wonderful people, and Cleve was a longtime friend of Ralph's.

One afternoon Ralph flew into Sedona, bringing two other men with him. One was Cleve Backster and the other was Phil Paul, who later bought the property now known as **Canyon del Oro**. This acreage has been hotly contested by a group who called it the Seven Canyon Development. Over the years, fighting over this land has gone on and on, with many old-timers still contesting its development. The whole matter is cussed and discussed, and the outcome is in limbo at this time.

As we visited together that afternoon, Cleve told us about his early research. One morning he had decided to have a couple of eggs for breakfast. All his eggs were connected to his lie detector machine, and when he thought of cooking them, he observed a strange thing happen. The screen showed the vibration of the eggs stopping dead still, as if they had all fainted at his thought of putting them into boiling water. Needless to say, he was amazed at how sensitive they were to his thoughts, and he didn't have eggs for breakfast that morning.

I was familiar with Cleve's research and was excited at meeting him and hearing him tell of his experiments. As usual, I acted as a guide to show my visitors some of Sedona's most famous scenic areas. In the middle of the afternoon, Cleve said, "If you want to get a group of friends together, I would be happy to show my slides and talk about my ongoing research."

I was really enthusiastic about this possibility, so I stopped at my office to make a few calls to see if anyone would be interested. Wow, were they ever! I got some very positive response and began to see that my little church lecture room was not going to be adequate.

I had a rather simple and unique way of getting a crowd together. I kept a guest book with many names in it, and I routinely put a red dot beside those interested in psychic phenomena, a blue dot beside names of those who were interested in lectures on health, a green dot beside those interested in astrology and numerology and so on. Sometimes I would have two colored dots beside a name, which meant that person was interested in various New Age things.

By calling a few key people, I could quickly find out if there was enough interest in a subject. I also knew the leaders of many little groups. So by calling them first and asking if they would call their group and let their people know what would be happening, I saved time and didn't have to make so many calls.

When I called Dale Batesol, who at that time was the minister of the Unity Church, he was so excited at the prospect of hearing Cleve speak that he offered *his* church, which held approximately eighty-five people. He even offered to call the members of his congregation and alert them to the meeting. He told me that he had used Cleve's work many times in his sermons to illustrate how all life was one and interconnected.

In a few hours the evening was set up and things were rolling along nicely. The four of us had dinner and went to the church at 7:30 p.m. to set up Cleve's projector and screen. People started pouring in until the church was more than filled. Cleve's talk was enthusiastically received and all of us felt the evening was a huge success. He later told me he had many lecture commitments in South American cities where people were far more interested in his work than they were in the United States, so he was pleasantly surprised at how many Sedonans had been aware of his work. Even way back then (about thirty-five years ago) we had many aware and highly evolved citizens.

I later visited with Cleve Backster in San Diego, his home base, where he had a police academy and trained men in the police department to use lie detectors. At that time he worked many hours at night on his ongoing research because he said the vibrations at night were much more peaceful and it was easier to concentrate on his work. Unfortunately, a few years later his lie detector work was put out of business when Ted Kennedy had the use of lie detectors outlawed in court. If you are familiar with Kennedy's life story, you can well imagine why he did this.

I had some wonderfully interesting experiences whenever I visited Cleve. One time he had me sit beside a yogurt culture that was hooked up to his lie detector so that the vibes from the culture were projected on a screen. Suddenly he shot a question at me: "Have you overcome your mother's death?" She had passed on a year before that, and I started to say yes when I looked at the screen and saw the even lines of the yogurt culture suddenly making radical changes, shooting up and down on the screen. I hesitated, then answered, "Obviously not."

He then turned on his television and said he wanted me to watch *Roots* with him. I said, "No, I don't like that program. It is too violent." He replied, "That's why I want you to watch it, to see how your emotions react with the yogurt culture."

To my consternation, as we watched the movie, I saw the line on the yogurt screen violently going up and down. I could readily see how little control I had over my emotions while watching television — a thought-provoking little exercise.

I was fortunate to have many other fascinating experiences with Cleve's research. His latest research is discussed in Robert B. Stone's fascinating book, *The Secret Life of Your Cells*. Cleve's work helped me see how every living thing is interconnected — even the lowly yogurt culture knew what I was feeling. How many other things, such as trees, plants and animals, are also tuned in to our emotional being? I now believe that all life, even our house, our car and other so-called inanimate objects, reacts to our emotions.

If we want to be a master, we had better learn emotional control. Not stop our emotions, but direct them into loving and benign vibrations so we can be at harmony and oneness with all things, animate and inanimate. Haven't you noticed how a car that is kicked and cussed at breaks down often, whereas vehicles that are loved, given praise and thanks, maybe even a friendly pat now and then, very seldom have problems?

For years I have not allowed anyone to fight and argue or otherwise put their negativity into my home. I open the door and direct them outside to vent their anger. Because of this, many sensitive friends notice that my house has a feeling of great peace and tranquillity.

21

Three Special Ladies

Heather and Sedona's First
Metaphysical Magazine . . .

*A*mong the many remarkable women I knew and
admired from my early days in Sedona is Heather
Hughes, who published Sedona's first metaphysical
magazine. *Sedona Life* was a beautiful magazine with
gorgeous colored photographs of the red rock country.
Unfortunately, it was too far ahead of its time and went
out of business after a few years.

When Heather married she moved to a large ranch in
Big Sur, California, and became a well-known guru. She
taught, gave seminars and lectures and wrote *The
Sedona Trilogy*, which is delightful.

Eventually she moved to Cottonwood, Arizona,
where she continued her work in the field of metaphys-
ics. I hadn't heard from her for about ten years when
she phoned to ask me to lunch at the **Café and Salad
Bar**.

We had a wonderful visit, talking about old times

and catching up with each other. After our luncheon she asked, "Would you like to see my white wolf? She is out in my van." So we went out to the parking lot. Heather opened the van's sliding door, and there stood this big white wolf who looked directly into my eyes with a steady, penetrating gaze that held us both for a long, long moment.

Heather remarked in surprise, "I can't believe this! She never allows anybody to look into her eyes." I told her I had a very strong feeling that this wolf and I knew each other on a soul level.

That was the last time I heard from Heather. She moved again and I lost track, but from time to time I've heard that she is giving seminars around the country.

Lucy and My Flirty Eyes . . .

My first metaphysical girlfriend was Lucy, a tall girl who was a lot of fun and was very wise. We were buddies for many years and often traveled together in my motor home. She had a ne'er-do-well sort of husband who never seemed to find work that suited him. One day Lucy told me, "I'm going to try beaning him to death; maybe he'll leave." So she fed him beans for breakfast, lunch and dinner. One day she said to me in disgust, "He loves it! Guess the only way out is divorce." Later she did get a divorce.

I used to have my ten o'clock coffee at the Goldust Café, which was in the middle of our little uptown area. Lucy was the fry cook there, and I would sit at the counter observing her in that dark and dismal kitchen, engulfed in an atmosphere of grease fumes. Sometimes when she wasn't busy, she would join me for coffee at the counter.

One day I said, with tears in my eyes, "I wish you didn't have to slave over a greasy stove." Lucy smiled and said something I had never heard of before. "Don't feel sorry for me. I'm paying off karma from a former life in England when I was a very wealthy woman. I was really a typical rich bitch — misusing my servants, being a snob and unfeeling to my family and friends. Now is my time to be the servant and experience humiliation. In my later life I will come into a fortune and have a chance to see if I've actually learned something." I was astounded at this revelation and lived to see it all come true.

Lucy and I had wonderful times together and I learned a lot from her. At one point I became annoyed with her because she was always saying, "I could care less." I heard her repeat these words so often, I really got irritated. One day I exploded and said, "If you say that again, I may push those words down your throat!"

Lucy grew very serious for a moment or two, then answered, "Funny thing is, I never say that unless I'm with you. I really have tried not to say it, but I open my mouth and out it comes. You must need it for some reason." I started to take a really good look at myself and began to realize she was right. I did care too much about what others thought and said about me. In other words, I cared too much about public opinion. I needed to "care less."

In later years when I was involved in all sorts of unorthodox activities, such as teaching yoga and hosting psychic lecturers and healers, I attracted heavy criticism from all directions. This was my chance to learn to care less about what people were saying about me. I seemed to have a deep sense of what I was supposed to be doing in Sedona, so I just shrugged my shoulders and went on doing what I was doing. It took a lot of courage and introspection and I often cried myself to sleep, but finally I really did learn to *care less*.

But to go on with Lucy's story: Eventually she went to work for a psychology professor at Northern Arizona University in Flagstaff. He owned several acres of land and two houses. He lived in one and Lucy lived in the other — a little stone guest house. For many years she cleaned house for the professor, cooked and did other chores. He was an interesting man and they became good friends — not a romance, but a wonderful friendly relationship.

He was a good hypnotist and several times he attempted to put Lucy and me into a hypnotic trance. He thought he could help me with the asthma problem. I trusted him and really hoped he could put me under. But both Lucy and I would lie there while he was doing the countdown and become more and more awake. We used to go to Helen Fry's place, and he would try to put all three of us into a trance for past-life recall. Helen was a wonderful subject and went under immediately, but Lucy and I didn't. We seemed to be resisting unconsciously and just lay there listening to Helen. What we heard was fascinating.

In one session she was a pilot on a ship in outer space. We found this especially interesting because she had married Jack Fry, who had started TWA many years before. He was a pilot and Helen flew all over the world with him. When they flew over Sedona, they were so drawn to the area of the red rocks that they purchased a large ranch. That is how Helen first came to Sedona.

She also told of her past life as a priest at Stonehenge. She described this ancient place in detail and mentioned how the sun penetrated through an opening in the rocks at a special time of year.

Much to everyone's surprise, when Lucy's friend and employer passed on, he left his entire estate to her. I remembered Lucy's story of a past life of riches, and I watched with great interest to see how this sudden wealth would affect her. Much to my horror and sadness, she appeared to revert right back to her "rich bitch" ways. She bought a baby-blue Thunderbird and drove around town with the windows down, smoking a cigarette in a long fancy holder. I could hardly believe that my good friend Lucy could let this happen again.

Shortly after this she left Sedona and went to Texas, where she had a son in the service. She was gone for four years. Then suddenly she came back to Sedona, bought a little house and settled down as the old Lucy I had known. Evidently she had come to terms with her karma during those four years, and this made me very happy for her. But she did not live long. She had lung cancer and passed on. Since childhood she had been a heavy smoker, and many times I had begged her to quit, but she would say, "I enjoy smoking and will not give it up."

My association with Lucy was a long one and was fulfilling in many ways. We often called each other and exchanged birthday gifts, using the same exotic purple ribbon we saved from year to year — one of my fondest memories of those days.

Lucy and I used to meditate together on a weekly basis. At that time she was house-sitting on an estate in the **Red Cliffs** area and had a large room with twin beds — which was great for us, because we both preferred to meditate lying down.

One day I was a little late in getting out there. When I walked in, I was grumbling about why I had to endure men chasing me around my desk. I was really disgusted and really angry. I told Lucy how I'd finally pulled my desk out toward the middle of the room so I would have an escape route in case I had another amorous client. That desk was a big heavy one, but I was so furious and so determined to provide myself an exit that I had actually managed to move it myself. "I do not understand why this keeps happening," I sputtered. "I am not a flirtatious person. I am always very businesslike, especially with men." Lucy just laughed and said, "You've got flirty eyes." I denied this vehemently.

Finally we lay down on our respective beds and settled down to meditate. When I got deeply into the alpha state, I suddenly saw a movie of myself. I was dressed in a harem costume, complete with flowing veil, and the eyes that looked out from my veiled face were definitely mine, and indeed, they *were* flirtatious! I realized that in those days the eyes were the only part of a woman that was allowed to be seen, and obviously I had learned very well how to project with mine. Apparently some of that ability still lingered in my eyes on a subconscious level. I sat up and cried out, "Lucy, you were right!"

We had a good laugh together about my flirty eyes, and after that I was even more cautious about being friendly with my eyes. Today, some people seem to think I am too aloof. Maybe I overdo it.

Jane and Seeing into Another Dimension . . .

Jane was another fascinating person I met while I was still living on the **Upper Red Rock Loop Road**. In fact, she is probably the most interesting human being I have ever known. My dear friend Ralph Bergstresser was also a friend of hers, and it was he who brought us together. I will never forget our first meeting on Highway 89A, where I had parked awaiting her prearranged arrival.

As she drove up, got out of her car and walked toward me, I had the distinct impression of — perhaps I should say, I had a vision of — Napoleon Bonaparte walking toward me. Later, when I knew her well, I came to believe that she might have been Napoleon in a past incarnation or at least very close to him.

What a fascinating lady she was! Her intellect was far above average and she shared many of her insights and experiences with me. She had just suffered a fire that had destroyed not only her home, but also all her treasures and records — everything she owned. Her insurance was not in effect at the time, for she was just moving into this new house when the fire occurred.

At the time we met, she was not only in shock, but also sick and broke. I told her she could live with me until she got on her feet. She was smart and resourceful and had many talents, so I knew she would get herself together in a short time. Jane stayed with me for about a year, and what a delightful companion she was!

She could see spirits and often regaled me with tales of the strange entities she saw as she came and went on her trips up and down the Loop Road. Often she saw pioneer persons who also saw her! Her various psychic abilities were extremely unusual, and during that year together I found life pretty exciting.

I learned about elves, fairies, devas and guides. As time went on she seemed to become more and more aware of the invisible (to me) world around us. She would speak of an elderly oriental gentleman who often joined us. Dressed in rich brocades, he would sit on the sofa, but try as I might, I could not see him. When Jane described him she always remarked, "He looks so sad, so very sad." Finally I suggested that she ask him why he was sad, and her answer was, "He is sad because he is your guide and you don't pay any attention to him."

After this the three of us began a three-way conversation. We would ask him questions we had written ahead of time. I would read the questions, Jane would tell me what he said, and I would write down his answers. I found all this truly enlightening. We kept a notebook of these questions and answers and learned much from this oriental gentleman. When Jane left, she took the notebook with her, so I have no record of these conversations.

One morning at breakfast, Jane suddenly started to see into my body. She was startled to find that she was looking into my chest, and she told me what she saw. Being an asthmatic, my lungs were not operating very efficiently and did not look too great.

When she came home that evening after a day's work selling time-shares in a mobile home park, she seemed quite shaken by what had happened that day. She had been seeing into the bodies of clients and those she met. She said it was terrible to see the things wrong with their bodies; she found this to be a definite distraction. I suggested that she tune it out and see these things only when she wanted to and concentrated purposefully on a specific person. Eventually she did work this out and was able to do her work and be around others without this disturbing phenomenon.

One afternoon as she arrived home and got out of her car, she saw that a large bush beside my back door was alive with fairies. She was so excited, and described them to me as being every color of the rainbow. Much to her distress, two of the fairies had followed her into the house and were beating against the window trying to get out. Both of us thought that fairies should be able to go right through a window, but apparently not these fairies. Jane opened the door and managed to shoo them out.

Often she saw a comical little elf on my back patio. She told me he was about eighteen inches tall and was dressed like a typical elf. The little fellow could talk, but he talked so fast that Jane couldn't figure out what he was saying. They began to have conversations together, using sign language. He told her he was ten thousand years old and lived under the bridge that spanned a wide ditch running through my property. He said he was a guard for that area. Jane began to call him Sammy.

When I first got up in the morning, I usually did some yoga exercises on my patio. Jane usually slept late and was seldom up and about when I was doing my morning thing. She would phone me later in the day and tell me exactly what postures and exercises I had performed that morning. Sammy had shown her everything I'd done, and he was always absolutely right. It was then I began to believe he was a real entity out there.

One evening Jane and I were talking about Sammy and wondering where he went at night. We also speculated about where fairies went after dark. Neither of us came up with any convincing answers, so for the moment we abandoned our speculations about the fairy kingdom and turned on the television to hear one of Pavarotti's wonderful concerts.

The next morning there was Sammy out on the back patio, showing Jane what he had seen on television the night before. He was imitating the great Pavarotti —

every gesture, every posture, even the familiar bow with handkerchief in hand. We knew then that Sammy was around after dark and decided that the fairies were, too.

One day Jane and I drove up to Flagstaff to spend the night at Little America. About halfway up the canyon, Jane told me that Sammy was sitting on the back seat. Although she didn't say so, I had the impression that she was a bit uneasy about Sammy going so far from home. While we were having dinner in the coffee shop, he sat on a shelf above us, but when we went to our room, Sammy wasn't with us.

Jane became very upset, fearing that he might be lost in this unfamiliar place. She kept going outside to look for him, calling his name. He didn't show up. I told her not to worry because I was certain that he needed no transportation and would just go back home. But Jane was still uneasy.

When we arrived home in Sedona the next afternoon, there was Sammy on the patio. Jane was much relieved, for she had become quite fond of the little fellow.

I would often come home late after Jane had gone to bed, and I could hear her talking in her sleep. In the morning she didn't remember anything about it and wanted to know what was going on, so we decided I would open her door a crack and write down what she said. I would stand in the hall with a notebook, scribbling down her conversations, and the next day she would read my notes.

One night I heard her arguing with someone who was trying to persuade her to go somewhere. She kept saying, "No, I'm tired. I had a hard day and I want to sleep!" The argument went on and on. She was very definite and determined, but apparently the persons she was talking to were even more determined. Finally, Jane said, "Okay, okay! Just let me sleep a couple of hours and then I'll go with you."

The next day she had no recollection of her night's adventure, but reading my notes triggered her memory. She told me that she went to another planet where she was well-known. Some kind of ceremony was being held in her honor, and she was presented with a special medallion on a chain, which she described in detail.

Jane was one of those rather rare people who see auras clearly. In the evening she often accompanied me to hear the latest channeling going on in my building. She told me that she could tell a fake channeler by his aura.

If the channeler's aura did not change color when the entity came into his body, he was either an impostor or was channeling himself. Of course, it is possible for a person to be channeling himself and have no idea that the words he speaks are his own and not those of some spirit entity, so these channelers are charlatans unaware.

As we sat in the audience, listening to the latest channeler, she would often look over at me and shake her head. Then I would know this was another channeler who just didn't check out. In those days I was checking out everything, so this was a pretty good education for me, learning what was real and what was not.

At that time Ramtha was very popular and gave a weekend seminar in Phoenix. We both went, of course. Jane remarked that if J.Z. Knight's aura did not change, she would just get up and walk out, even if she *had* paid $300 for the session. I watched as Ramtha slipped into the body of J.Z. Knight and then saw that Jane was glued to her seat, clearly having no intention of leaving. Jane stayed for the entire event and told me later that the change in J.Z.'s aura was dramatic. When Ramtha took over, his aura was an electric-blue spiral that went right through the ceiling. We went to hear Ramtha another time, and Jane described the same electric-blue spiral.

I delved into the many remarkable gifts Jane possessed, and this was another period of learning for me. I believe our best gurus are our friends and family, from whom we can learn so much if we are alert and open to the lessons they bring us. Jane often remarked that she was grateful I could understand her strange and extraordinary gifts instead of thinking she was ready for the booby hatch.

When a person has abilities like this, he may lead a lonely life because he cannot talk freely about what he sees for fear of ridicule. Even though I seem to have put this type of psychic ability on the shelf this lifetime, I know these things are very real, and I am open to them without any hesitation. You can't get too far out for me.

22

Unconventional Healers

Nameless One . . .

Over the years many famous and wonderful healers have come to visit Sedona. A few fall in love with the area and come back to live here. The first healer to come to my attention (who shall be nameless) was considered really far-out, not the least bit spiritual, and he made some rather extravagant claims. So, tongue in cheek, I thought, "Let's see what he can do," and I gave him a chance to prove his claims. I invited him to my church to demonstrate his healing ability.

About twenty people showed up to experience a healing. I watched in amazement as he managed to heal almost every problem the audience gave him.

First he lay down on a couch and proceeded to build up energy with some special kind of breathing. Then he went to each person and asked what the problem was. One person complained of an ulcerated tooth that was throbbing. The pain stopped completely when he passed his hands over the painful area, and when I checked with her several months later, her tooth was still pain-free.

One lady was wearing a neck brace and was in great pain as a result of a car accident. He told her to take off the brace, and he tossed it into a corner, saying she wouldn't need it again. Interestingly enough, she didn't.

I had a nagging pain in my foot that had been bothering me for months. A few passes over my foot with his hand, and the pain was gone. It never came back. Needless to say, I was impressed in spite of my skepticism.

However, my admiration waned when he propositioned me. I said, "I thought you had a wife in Prescott," and he said, "Yes, I do. But she's my Prescott wife and I'd like you to be my Sedona wife." I told him to go back to his wife and "forget it!" He probably had wives all over the country. I guess I was supposed to be flattered, but I was not.

I never saw or heard of this wonderful healer again.

Mietek Wirkus . . .

More miracles were performed by the healers Mietek Wirkus and his wife Margaret who came to Sedona from behind the Iron Curtain in Poland. He called his healing method "bio-energy healing," and he removed energy blocks from diseased organs, thus allowing his patients the opportunity to heal themselves. He was marvelous, and was the most humble man I've ever known. He had a Christ-like personality and was full of impersonal, unconditional love. One morning at breakfast I asked Mietek if he had come into this life with that humble attitude or if he had worked to acquire it.

He told me he was born with this gift.

The first evening at my church he did a series of mini healings for each of the people who attended. I watched carefully as he walked through the audience, treating those who needed help. He would pass his hands around the head and shoulders of his subjects, not touching, but working a few inches away from the body. He came to one woman who apparently needed something different, and I noticed he worked about a foot above her head. Later I asked him why he had given her a different treatment. He could speak very little English at that time, and his wife interpreted his answer for me. He said that this woman was a channel who often worked with the spirits of the dead, and she had some rather unpleasant astral conditions he was attempting to correct. I found this fascinating.

Later, I was delighted to discover that whenever I was with Mietek I had no asthma, but when we were apart the asthma was as bad as ever. I told him I wished I could keep him in my pocket so I would have no breathing problem. He told me that even when he was a child, his presence did the same for his asthmatic sister. He also mentioned that his schoolteachers noticed that when he was in a classroom, all was peaceful and harmonious, but as soon as he left the room, the children became their normal restless and agitated selves. So even as a child, he was different and special.

In one of his seminars he told the group that years before in Europe, he had met five monks who were traveling about teaching a special breathing technique for healing to highly evolved people they met on their travels. It was this technique Mietek used to heal, and he attempted to teach us how to do it. Sorry, but I just didn't get it.

The Wirkuses now live in Bethesda, Maryland, teaching classes for doctors, nurses and laymen. Mietek was selected as one of the top ten world sensitives to work with the Menninger Foundation on a project being carried out in a copper-lined room. He is also involved in other research projects at a scientific foundation in Boston and in publishing his reports in scientific journals. In spite of their busy schedules, the Wirkuses occasionally found time to revisit Sedona, but I haven't seen them lately.

Dr. Fred Houston . . .

About thirty years ago Dr. and Mrs. Francis Houston, whom I had heard about from a friend, stopped in Sedona to visit me, and there began a long and special friendship. Dr. Fred had been a practicing chiropractor for at least forty years, and a very successful one. Every summer for twenty years he had traveled across the United States teaching and healing. He was on his way back to California after one of these summer trips when he first visited Sedona. He immediately knew he wanted to live here, but his wife was happy in their Pine Valley home and didn't want to move. When she passed on twenty years ago, here he came, bag and baggage, to follow his twenty-year dream to live in Sedona.

At ninety years of age Doc is still practicing, scheduling seminars and sharing his tremendous knowledge of the healing arts. He is the author of the book *The Healing Benefits of Acupressure*, which helps you to heal yourself using pressure points. He is also a Doctor of Divinity and does a type of spiritual healing that includes pressure points, balancing body energies and getting rid of negative entities. I have been privileged to observe many of his healings; even some people who had been given up as incurable have been healed miraculously by Doctor Fred. He puts great emphasis on using your own body's "powerful resources to restore, preserve and enhance vital good health."

Doctor Fred is a wizard with herbs and, guided by spirit, he prepares his herbal formulas and dispenses them along with his special brand of wit, wisdom and compassion. His spontaneous laughter and joy of life are catching, and if he is a bit cantankerous from time to time, surely he is entitled.

Doctor Fred lives alone except for a constant stream of admiring visitors, and continues to see patients, working his magic in his own unorthodox way using acupressure and his unique herbal mixtures. The famous herbalist, Hanna Kroeger, once wrote of him as one of the most important healers of our time.

Doc Brown . . .

Another of Sedona's unusual and fascinating healers is Bill Brown, an etheric surgeon, one of only a few in the whole world. I consider him to be one of Sedona's miracle workers. He is a quiet, unassuming man who seldom speaks about what he does. Over the years I had read about him in several books on healers and healing and had hoped I would meet him some day.

One weekend a mutual friend from Hollywood came to spend a few days with me and brought this wonderful man with him. We arranged for two etheric operations to be performed in the old Keller Building. We had found a person to act as nurse. Doc is completely in a trance during an operation, working with twenty-three doctors on the other side of the veil, so he must have someone assist him on this side.

Somehow there was a misunderstanding about time, and the assistant didn't show up. The patient was on the table waiting and I was suddenly pressed into service as the nurse. If I had not witnessed this remarkable event, I would never have believed what took place. It was absolutely phenomenal. However, seeing is believing, and I was privileged to see some astounding miracles of healing that day.

A truly gifted man, Bill Brown also has the ability of inner knowing. In his younger days he counseled many people, including Hollywood stars. He and his late wife, Maria, moved to Sedona about eighteen years ago and purchased the very same house I had originally built for my mother. Now, retired from his healing work, he continues to live in Sedona pursuing his vast interests in radionics.

I realize that much of this may sound just too far out for some of you. However, marvelous and inexplicable things do occur in this world of ours, and Dr. Brown is closely in touch with many of our mysteries.

Shortly before I completed the manuscript for this book, my old friend Bill Brown passed on. He went quietly, with no newspaper announcement and no funeral. Perhaps he has gone to Arcturus, where he will be better understood than he was by his contemporaries, for life is not always easy for those who march to a different drummer.

I'd like to tell about his early life, when as a little boy he used to wander in the Georgia woods to visit a "very large Indian" he'd met there. This Indian was sort of like his guardian angel or guide from the spirit world, but to Bill he was "absolutely real." The Indian taught the child about healing herbs and about nature, and spoke of invisible phenomena.

The years passed, and Bill became a talented musician, planning a career as a concert violinist. However, the time came when his old Indian friend told him that he could not pursue his musical career in this lifetime. The Indian explained that Bill had spent four previous lifetimes preparing for this present life as an etheric surgeon, and he introduced the twenty-three etheric doctors who were to work with him.

Reluctantly, Bill gave up his plans for a musical career and allowed his psychic abilities to expand. Soon he was traveling all over the United States, treating and healing as he went. He bought an old WWII plane, refurbished it to top condition, and criss-crossed the country to go to those who needed his help. By now he was a famous healer, and calls came from everywhere.

At that time Bill's first wife acted as nurse, and she went with him wherever he was called. After she died, he continued his etheric operations, usually asking a "healer" or doctor to act as nurse. But he was very lonely and missed his wife terribly. He was a lost soul without her.

The time Bill asked me to stand in for the "nurse" who didn't show up, I had no idea what I was getting into. One of the surgeons from the other side was upset with me because I couldn't hold a patient's head still (as he had ordered) and take notes at the same time. He had said the patient must not move her head while he was operating. She was bobbing her head up and down and all around and I was using every bit of my strength trying to keep her head still. No way could I be taking notes. In his opinion I was a total failure, and he angrily said, "I thought you were a nurse!"

"No! I'm *not* a nurse. I'm just filling in for the nurse who hasn't shown up," I explained. After that he was a little easier on me.

Bill saw two patients that day, and I observed that each one had to be helped from the operating table to her car. Both had been told that they must have a driver waiting and a place to recuperate for two weeks. The doctor gave strict instructions for their convalescent care. These ladies told me they felt very weak, as if they'd had a "real" operation. After their recovery each of them told me she'd had a wonderfully successful "surgery" and her medical problem had been solved.

Later, after Bill and Maria had moved to Sedona, I was the first patient he operated on. Maria was well-prepared to work with Bill as a nurse, and *she* took notes.

When my operation was being scheduled, I had asked Bill if he would allow Lou Van Alts, the healing minister from my church, to be there. Bill was incensed and said, "What do you think this is, a sideshow?" But after thinking about it, he agreed to let Lou observe, for Lou was a fine healer in his own right and was really interested in Bill's procedures.

I was told I would not be able to drive after the operation, and my friend Laura Bauer drove me there and took me home with her to recuperate.

When I was ready on the operating table, Bill sat down on a chair in the corner of the room and appeared to go into a meditative state. After a few minutes, he suddenly collapsed and slumped forward over his knees. It was as if he had completely left his body, just emptied it and left it there. He stayed in this position for a minute or two, then abruptly sat straight up and said, "Top o' th' mornin' to ya" in a strong Irish brogue.

Maria introduced this doctor by name and told us he was the diagnostician. The doctor (in Bill's body) energetically left his chair, came over to me and moved his right hand about two inches above my entire body.

"You have a leaky faucet, don't you?" I admitted that I did. "We'll fix that," he said, and continued with his diagnosis. At one point he said, "You like cheese, don't you?" When I answered yes, he remarked, "Cheese fouls up your arteries. You must never eat cheese again." To this day, I am careful not to eat cheese.

When he had finished my diagnosis, the doctor went back to the chair. Bill slumped over again. After a wait of a few more minutes, another doctor came into Bill's body. Bill sat up and became an entirely different person, with a different voice and different manner. If I had not been there, I never would have believed what was happening.

This doctor told us that he was going to anesthetize me. He asked Laura and Lou to feel my pulse and they reported that it was strong. Not touching me, he then appeared to plunge a needle into my neck, and I felt myself slipping away. He asked the two observers to feel my pulse again, and they both said there was almost no pulse. As for me, I still (more or less) knew what was going on, but felt anesthetized and in no pain.

I won't go into detail, but after each doctor completed his surgery, he would go out of Bill's body. Bill would collapse again and an entirely new specialist would take over his body, be introduced, do his work and leave.

The doctors had decided that I needed five operations right then and there. Later I was told that having five operations all at once was extremely unusual. Five separate times a different surgeon came, operated and left, each one with a distinctly different personality, voice and body language. Amazing! I could not have believed this had I not gone through it myself. No matter who might tell me about it, I would not, could not, have believed what happened that afternoon.

After my five operations, I was taken to the recovery room for a couple of hours and then home with Laura and put to bed. It took me awhile to recover because so many things had been fixed, but when it was all over, everything was fine — even my leaky faucet.

One time I asked Bill, "Where do you go when you are out of your body?"

"Back to my home planet," he said. "To Arcturus. I just hate coming back here!" So I figure that's where he is.

Believe this story or not, all of it actually happened. I was there.

Dr. Stephen Chang . . .

In 1978 I attended a seminar on methods of alternative healing held at **Poco Diablo** in Sedona. The speaker was the brilliant Dr. Stephen T. Chang, a new arrival from China who was living and teaching in San Francisco. Today he is invited to lecture all over the world, travels extensively and is the author of several books on his special interests and studies of the Tao, I Ching, acupuncture, acupressure, exercise and diet.

In the seventies, Chinese medicine was little known in this country, and the Sedonans who gathered for the seminar didn't quite know what to expect. Dr. Chang turned out to be charming, gracious and a fascinating lecturer in spite of some difficulty with the English language. He was enormously knowledgeable, easily translating information from ancient Chinese texts, and relating unusual case histories from his own experience as well as from 6000-year-old records of Chinese medical practices.

He had his audience hanging on every word, and then, quite innocently, I think, he flung himself on the floor and illustrated the man's and then the woman's positions for fulfilling the sex act according to the holy teachings of the Tao. After each demonstration he would shoot a question at me, "Are you taking notes?" Needless to say, I couldn't think of any good reason to do so.

He told us that in order to have a healthy body and cure our ailments, we must practice these positions with a partner twelve times a day for two weeks! He taught a certain position for each different ailment. In a moment of bravado, one woman in her eighties asked, "At my age, where would I find a willing and able partner?" Dr. Chang's answer was, "Oh, that should be no problem."

Well, we white-haired, small-town Sedonans were not as sophisticated in those days as his San Francisco audiences must have been, and we certainly were not accustomed to such graphic and open discussions of sex. If we were not shocked, we were at least mightily surprised.

You may be sure this seminar was not soon forgotten.

A New Breed . . .

All manner of nontraditional healers are attracted to

Sedona. Some are legitimate and some, I'm sorry to say, are not, although their brochures and publicity may proclaim them to be the world's greatest. I have met dozens of serious healers and bodyworkers and been introduced to a wide variety of healing techniques, procedures and New Age energy devices.

I have experienced hands-off and hands-on, and I have long been familiar with the healing power of prayer, which certainly is no New Age discovery. I've investigated many an herb, lotion, salve, potion, pill, tablet, liquid and powder that have been energized, potentized, magnetized and infused with the healing essences of nature, of love and of the universe.

I have tried magnetic mattresses (very uncomfortable), pillows, belts and patches as well as crystals, stones, magnets, muds and various "machines" of an electrical, mechanical or radionic nature. Although nothing so far has helped my asthma much, I have witnessed many others who have been healed of various serious conditions.

Both new and old "natural" healing treatments constantly keep cropping up in Sedona. I've welcomed some and discarded others, but I have tried them all. I have learned that what works for one may not work for another. As long as the human desire for physical, mental, emotional and spiritual health is with us, I expect Sedona residents will be among the first to embrace dedicated healers and their offerings of hope for relief of pain and illness.

So far I have mentioned only a few of the many, many early unorthodox healers I've known in Sedona, but times are changing and a new breed of healers has moved into our lives. Science and spirit long have avoided each other like the plague, but there is an increasingly strong movement afoot to accept, or at least investigate, the healing benefits offered by the combined efforts of the traditional physician and the spiritual mystic.

I find it encouraging that the general public is showing an intense and robust desire to embrace alternative and complementary medical procedures. The interest in supplementary medical health, with emphasis on the whole person, is growing. I am delighted to see that books on health by Andrew Weil, Deepak Chopra and Caroline Myss are selling like crazy. Generally speaking, these doctors are telling us that the whole person must be treated, not just the symptom. When the body is ailing, the mind and spirit must be treated as well.

Keith Boericke . . .

Keith Alexes Boericke, one of the pioneers in this "new" emphasis on energy healing for the whole body, is a gifted and experienced man of vision who moved to Sedona over ten years ago. A nationally licensed acupuncturist and oriental herbalist by training (L.Ac.), he has chosen to treat the physical body not only with traditional acupuncture and oriental herbal combinations, but also with his own system of Body Mystica Healing and Counseling.

"I look at the 'form behind the form,'" says Keith. "I contact the body-spirit energies in my patient's body to determine if the spirit energies are communicating well with each other. Inharmonious body-spirit communication can lead to dis-ease of the patient's physical, mental and emotional bodies. This process actively involves the patient in his own healing through understanding the emotional and mental energy patterns that may be affecting his health."

Keith's specialty is his mystical ability to identify negative energy carried over from past lives and to demonstrate how this negativity is working against the patient in creating ill health. He has been an ordained minister for twenty years and a professional astrological/ spiritual counselor for over thirty years, using astrology and information from the akashic records to facilitate healing. He utilizes imagery, color and sound as well as acupressure, acupuncture and herbal therapy, if necessary, to assist his patients in bringing balance and healing into their lives.

His Body Mystica is a "new" way for healers and bodyworkers to look at the complexity of health problems facing them. He represents the growing group of healers who are actively and successfully bridging body-mind-spirit healing.

He, like so many fine healers before him, is a modest man, not one to blow his own horn. In a way I consider him to be one of Sedona's best-kept secrets in the field of complementary healing.

23

Early Gurus

Tarthang Tulku Rinpoche . . .

I have always had a very strong desire to meet a Tibetan lama and thought I would have to go to Tibet to meet one. Little did I know thirty years ago that Sedona was such a magical place that anyone I had a great desire to meet would eventually wind up on my doorstep, so to speak. I never had to leave Sedona to meet them.

One day four ladies from Scottsdale arrived at the Keller Building with a wonderful and very colorful Tibetan lama dressed in his native costume: a robe, bound legging boots, a little round skullcap — the works. These ladies, two of whom I had already met, were rescuing a few lamas from India, where they had escaped from Tibet during the Chinese invasion of their country. These women wanted to establish a monastery in the Western world and were looking Sedona over as a possible site. They eventually did establish such a place in Berkeley, California.

This lama was learning English very quickly and could communicate well. His name was Tarthang Tulku Rinpoche. He was a highly accomplished lama of the Nyingma tradition and the founder of several Tibetan centers and institutions in our country. He commented that Sedona reminded him of some of the areas in the Himalayas, and he felt very much at home here. He also added that he had lived in this vicinity fifty civilizations ago, which absolutely blew my mind. It had to have been eons ago.

The ladies asked if Sedona would like to have him give a three-day seminar. I gave my hearty approval and proceeded to make arrangements for a date two weeks ahead. Thirty people signed up; considering this was thirty years ago, this turnout was remarkable. Tarthang Tulku tried mightily to impart some of his wisdom and knowledge to us, but I must admit that most of it was way over our heads.

However, I did learn one remarkable lesson from him that will always stay with me. On the last day of the seminar he gave each of us a private consultation. One of my girlfriends was ahead of me. When she came out, she was radiant. She had told him she had two very strong desires — lots of sex and a great deal of money — and he had told her that it was okay to indulge these desires. I was shocked at the story and indignant that he would encourage her in these things.

My turn was next, and I told him much the opposite story; for I had lost all desire for sex at an age that did not seem quite natural and I had difficulty concentrating on making money. I made a good living, but my heart was not into making money. He smiled and said not to worry, as these things had left *me*; I had not tried to rid myself of *them*. He said it was the natural way to rid oneself of desires in this lifetime.

I then proceeded to reprimand him for giving my girlfriend the opposite advice. Rinpoche had a fat belly like a Buddha, and he laughed and laughed until it bounced up and down.

He said that because he was a person whom my friend respected and looked up to, had he told her these were bad things for her to do and that she must resist them, she could be fighting them for the rest of her life. As a result, the desires would become stronger and more difficult. He said that by telling her that her indulgence was all right, she would eventually become saturated, and these things would automatically drop away from her. She would overcome them in this lifetime.

I was astounded at his wisdom and never forgot this lesson. To fight a desire is to give it more strength and power. To indulge it weakens it, and eventually it will leave. I think this may also apply to many addictions the human race is plagued with. Perhaps you have to fall flat on your face and hit bottom before your addictions give you up.

So even way back then, Sedona was receiving wisdom from Tibet.

Disciple of Paramahansa Yogananda, Kriya Yoga and Tai Chi . . .

Sedona has been a real mecca for gurus. Over the years they have arrived and departed, some leaving a few followers behind — either disillusioned or heartbroken. Personally, I have received benefit from several of them, and I would like to tell about some of the wisdom I gained. Much of this wisdom was in learning what *not* to do. I will refrain from naming all these gurus; some of you will recognize their teachings.

I met one, a disciple of Paramahansa Yogananda, at a seminar in Phoenix and was initiated into kriya yoga. When I was being initiated, my eyes were closed, but I felt that whatever he was doing above my head was very powerful, because I felt the energy. I had the sensation that my head was about to explode, and tears streamed down my face. This was a very moving experience, to say the least.

After my initiation I faithfully practiced kriya. Kriya is a meditation ritual involving the breath and visualization, working with the body chakras. After three months of practice I began to have strong vibrational ripples down my spine whenever I heard the Truth. This was rather unsettling to me. By now my teacher was out of town, so I had no one to talk to about this. I already felt I was a pretty kooky lady, and I knew that at times some of my friends thought I was really a bit strange. So I quit my kriya rituals at once, thinking that since I still had to make my living at my business, I could not allow myself to be too odd.

Two years later my teacher came back to Sedona and I attended another of his seminars. I told him what had happened and that I had stopped practicing kriya. He said, "You should not have stopped. You were just beginning to make progress." For ten years I continued to read his books and attend every one of his seminars.

One in Bishop, New Mexico, was especially interesting. At this seminar we were to spend twenty-four hours without speaking, which was a new idea for many of us. I was with a girlfriend and we agreed not to speak for the twenty-four hours. We took long walks in the wooded area adjacent to the lodge where we were staying. We read, ate our meals and attempted to do our normal routines without speaking. Both of us were completely comfortable with our silence. If we needed to communicate, we wrote each other notes. The next day we heard that several pairs of friends wound up screaming at each other; some had even gotten hysterical, and a few had to leave.

We also had lessons in t'ai chi chih from Justin F. Stone, author of *Tai Chi Chih, Joy Through Movement*. In t'ai chi chih there are eighteen movements, easy to learn and quickly beneficial. This popular instructor also teaches the 108 movements of t'ai chi ch'uan, which is more complicated and difficult to learn than are the eighteen movements he taught us. I truly enjoyed his class and have realized the benefits, including increased energy and a sense of well-being and joy.

It was at this seminar that I observed our guru drinking beer and being pretty chummy with the girls. At the time, I was terribly disillusioned and shocked and, sorry to say, judgmental. Later, when I learned that this young man had been a celibate monk since he was eighteen, I realized that he probably had a lot of catching up to take care of.

The Romantic Guru . . .

One of the memorable gurus who made his mark in Sedona's early days had a penchant for alcohol and for romance with a capital R. He was attractive, well-educated and a fascinating speaker who occasionally spoke in my church. Of course, the girls adored him.

I knew this young man had great promise because he was extremely talented and had a wonderful personality as well. I did all I could to help him, and he often spent weekends at my place. If I tried to give him advice about his behavior, he would curtly inform me that he didn't need a mother. The time came when I told him that as long as he partied and hung out with questionable companions, he could not stay at my house. Of course, this made him very angry with me.

It wasn't until the months went by that I found out the extent of his romantic escapades. Girls would come to cry on my shoulder and tell me about their love for him, their seduction and disillusionment. In time I heard many of these sad tales and began to see the repeated pattern in his method of seduction. It was always the same. He told them that because he had spent so many years in meditation and spiritual states, his semen was holy. If he deposited that semen in them, he told the girls, they would advance spiritually very quickly. If it hadn't caused so much heartbreak, this oft-repeated tale would be almost hilarious in its implications.

Many years later, looking back on all this activity with more wisdom and understanding, I began to think his romantic episodes were most likely needed by the girls so involved. Perhaps they needed the experience of heartbreak and disillusionment to advance their evolution or spiritual growth. It is often true that great heartbreak leads to a deeper opening of the heart chakra, and certainly those girls did gain *some* wisdom, so the experience wasn't all bad. I tell this story as a warning to some of you starry-eyed young women. Do not be so easily misled.

I also realized that even a playboy guru could be capable of good work. Who knows? That may have been his purpose in life, but I knew he was really capable of being a great spiritual leader. What a waste!

Teachings of Sri Aurobindo . . .

During my many years in Sedona, it has been my pleasure and my experience to meet many extremely interesting, talented and mostly highly evolved people. Some of these were also very intelligent, but at the same time rather eccentric. I remember one guru in particular who was a genius bordering at times almost on madness. He was talented in so many ways that if you could overlook his rather unusual actions, you would find he was full of information.

This guru was a student and follower of Sri Aurobindo and Mother Mira. I was fascinated with his extensive knowledge because I had been involved with the Aurobindo Center and the Aurobindo teachings for fifteen years. These teachings were not well-known in this country and I seldom found anyone who was truly knowledgeable on the subject. I had read every book Sri Aurobindo had written as well as the books written about him. And I had studied and attended classes faithfully, but still was not able to understand completely. Nevertheless I was deeply drawn to the Aurobindo philosophy and knew something important was there for me.

When I met this young teacher who was so knowledgeable, having spent several years in Pondicherry at Sri Aurobindo's ashram studying with Aurobindo and Mother Mira, I knew I must study with him and learn more. He was an excellent teacher and encouraged his students, saying, "Try it. It works."

Sri Aurobindo is the only East Indian guru I know of who has taught philosophy at several universities in our country. In a couple of hundred years he will be a legend. I consider my studies of his philosophy to be one of the highlights of my life. I decided to learn all I could from this young teacher because he understood Sri Aurobindo's work better than anyone I had encountered. He wound up living in my house for about a year, and I learned a lot from him, including what and what not to do.

One of the most delightful things I learned was the silent walking meditation. At this time I was living on six and a half acres on Keller Lane just off Upper Red Rock Loop Road. It was a wonderful place because great old sycamore and willow trees grew there, and the woods were magical. I made a big circular path through those woods so I could walk in a never-ending circle.

A group of us would meet there in the morning and do an hour-long walking meditation, which was a deeply moving experience for all of us. We would walk in single file, keeping a space between us, and as we walked we silently repeated a long Sri Aurobindo mantra. We were entirely silent; not a word was spoken.

Since the woods were indwelled by various nature spirits and devas, it was like a little patch of enchanted forest. This is one of the memories of that time that I treasure fondly. Many years later a psychic visited me, and as she walked through the forest she remarked that she heard echoes of what seemed like mantras being chanted. The atmosphere still held the vibrations from the days of our walking meditations.

One of this guru's most valuable lessons, which I shall never forget, was when he taught us to view horror and violent movies without becoming involved or reacting to them. I saw more ghastly movies in that short time than I had seen in a lifetime, most of which I never would have considered going to see. He gave us a lengthy, involved mantra that we memorized and kept repeating silently while watching the film. He would sit behind us, and if one of us got involved emotionally with the picture he would tap us on the shoulder and whisper, "Get back to your mantra." He must have been able to see our auras in the darkness of the theater because he spotted our lapses instantly and brought it to our attention.

One day he took us to a movie house in Phoenix that was showing not one but three very scary films. We were to see all three of them during the afternoon and evening. It was sort of like a graduation exercise of this particular phase of his teaching. I was sure that Sri Aurobindo had never resorted to such violent ways to get his message across, for he was a very gentle person.

At the theater, two friends and I sat together and had progressed through two of the movies with flying colors and were ready to tackle the last and most violent one.

We went to the ticket window to purchase our tickets, but the girl at the window said, "You ladies don't want to see that one. It is so terrible that some people faint and some come out screaming. Wouldn't you rather see one of the others?"

We were a threesome of white-haired ladies, obviously senior citizens, and she must have been afraid we might have heart attacks. We kept insisting that we wanted to see that particular picture, so she finally called the manager, who also tried his best to dissuade us. But we would not give up, so, looking very worried, he reluctantly accompanied us to the door of the auditorium. Our guru had told us earlier that there was a great message in that picture and that it contained an excellent moral teaching. He told us to watch for the lessons in it, so we settled down, dutifully repeating our mantra.

I wish I could remember the name of that film, but for some reason it has evaded me. It was an interesting picture, but at times it really was horrible. The story was about a small group of people who had gone to a mountain searching for friends who had recently disappeared there. This mountain had been constructed to be a form of initiation where one would go into a tunnel and meet his worst fears, either to conquer them or be destroyed in the process.

The first to enter the tunnel into the mountain was a woman who was deathly afraid of worms and crawling things. She soon encountered a small caterpillar crawling toward her, and she panicked. She screamed and screamed while the little worm grew larger and larger until it filled the entire tunnel and then proceeded to chew her up into little pieces. Needless to say, this was a pretty bloody scene, with much screaming going on in the audience. Meanwhile we three sat serenely, saying our mantra and rather enjoying the message of the story.

The other members of the group in the movie went through their own particular brand of terror, each one succumbing to his worst fears, except the man who was confronted with his lower self, a being who looked very much like himself but gross and satanic. It was quite an intense battle, but he overcame his worst fear and also his opponent. He was the only one who lived to walk out of the tunnel.

As we exited the theater into the lobby, the anxious manager was standing by the door, certain that we also might have succumbed. Instead, we came out smiling and laughing about the intricacies of the story and rather amused at the manager's concern. I said to my friends, "Little does he know that these three little old ladies are really yogis in disguise."

In looking back on this rather bizarre experience, I must admit it had great value, because it taught us to control our emotions and to be able to look at any kind of chaos, tragedy or violence without reacting. This is a handy thing to know when reading all the bad news in the newspapers or on television. Anyone who can control his emotions could also be of valuable influence during times of emergency.

Another thing I learned from this guru was to overcome carsickness. When I was the driver, I was okay, but if someone else was in the driver's seat, I got sick. I couldn't even read a road map when the car was in motion.

One day a group of us were going up to Flagstaff in my car and the guru insisted that he do the driving. I did not feel a bit comfortable about this and mentioned my carsickness. He just settled himself in the driver's seat and said, "I will show you how to overcome it."

As we were going around the curves on the switchbacks, I felt the familiar malady. He instructed me to focus attention on my abdomen. Then I was to speak to my stomach as if it were an unruly child and slap it, saying, "Stop it! You must stop!" In the meantime, I was to keep my attention focused on my stomach. This maneuver seemed to work, but then he stopped the car, told me to sit in the back seat and handed me a book, saying, "Read." I was pretty upset by this, as a back seat on a mountain road was a no-no for me, and so was reading in a car.

I was horrified at the time, but tried to do what he said while we drove around the switchback turns, and of course I got sick. But I was persistent and was soon able to read while sitting in the back seat and riding the curvy canyon road between Sedona and Flagstaff. Strange as it may seem, his carsickness lesson worked for me.

He also taught me how to handle pain. "When you have a pain, just let it go as far as it will," he said. "Don't try to stop it. When it reaches its maximum, it stops." This takes discipline, but it helps you lose your fear of pain and allows you to feel that you are in control.

As I had anticipated, this guru was an excellent teacher of Sri Aurobindo's philosophy, and some mornings when we two sat at the breakfast table, I strongly sensed that Sri Aurobindo was overshadowing him.

But all was not joy and sunshine. I could always tell from his looks and manner when I was in for trouble. He could be really mean to me and his attitude then almost bordered on hate. He seemed to enjoy putting me down and humiliating me.

Interestingly enough, I always felt I was stronger than he was. No matter how cleverly mean and arrogant he was, I knew my will was not only his match, but even stronger than his. Perhaps that was his problem.

I could go on and on telling the things I learned from this guru and the humiliations I suffered at his hands, but it would not serve any purpose. The year I studied with him was a serious year of learning. Although I'd rather not, I will tell one more story about my experience with him because it could be helpful to some of you dear readers.

At one point this young man decided I needed to rid myself of all ego and attachment. I suppose this is something most of those on a spiritual path would like to accomplish in this lifetime, but what a harsh way he had to bring this about. It almost destroyed me.

He insisted that every morning for two weeks I should sit and say, "I am an ignorant imbecile" over and over for twenty minutes. I believe I must have wanted to accomplish the death of the ego, or I would not have gone along with this, because it was grossly self-punishing.

He was trying to have me accomplish in two weeks what usually would take a·lifetime. He didn't tell me his plan, but after two weeks of this and other equally humiliating treatments by him, I realized I had definitely had enough and asked him to leave.

This was a long and rather painful experience too, but I held my ground and said he must go. Alone at last, I realized that although I seemed to have overcome the ego and all attachments, I had also lost the will to live. I would still get dressed and faithfully go to my office, for I felt I owed it to my salespeople to carry on as usual. But I felt like a zombie.

One morning as I was getting ready to go to the office, I became aware that I was actually enjoying the process of putting on my makeup, choosing the right clothes and matching jewelry and shoes. When I realized this, I desperately clutched onto that little spark of enjoyment like a drowning man grabbing for a life raft.

I also realized that if I lost all ego and attachments, there was no real reason to go on living. This was really the lesson I learned from this experience. Something deep, deep inside me said I was not yet through with life. It was not time to leave. So I began searching for little enjoyments, no matter how small, and grasped and held onto them with all my strength and determination.

Don't ever let anyone tell you to relinquish all ego, because if you do, you won't have any good reason for staying alive. I now cherish some of my little attachments and thank God for them.

The Pink Prince . . .

In the early days many gurus were attracted to Sedona, just as they are today. They would come and they would go, and this still goes on. However, one stands out in my memory because he caused quite a stir in Sedona. He was the most colorful guru of them all, the "Pink Prince," Hirindrah Singh of India.

The Pink Prince and Mary Lou.

Hirindrah was visiting the A.R.E. Center in Phoenix when a young lady in their library asked if he had ever been to Sedona. He said he hadn't, but would like to see it. She then offered to take him up to the red rock country. He commented that he would be more than glad to speak at a church in Sedona, but it must be one that believed in all religions as one. She said, "Oh, that would be Mary Lou Keller's church, the Sedona Church of Light." She called me to arrange for a Sunday meeting.

The following Sunday, a group gathered at the Keller Building, having been duly advised of his visit. We were all waiting for him as he walked up the steps, and were amazed to see this handsome young man right out of an Arabian Night's fairy tale, dressed in his pink Indian-style suit and pink

Prince Hirindrah, the Pink Prince.

turban and his wonderful black beard and mustache. His stunning appearance alone was certain to attract attention, but he also had great charisma. Everyone hung on his every word — which, by the way, was spoken in perfect English.

Having been tutored by English governesses, the Pink Prince was well-educated, not only in his own Sikh religion, but also in the Christian religion. His talks on Jesus were delightful, and everyone kept encouraging him to continue speaking. He had also made a study of the major religions of the world and could speak eloquently on any of them, so he became a favorite with the little Sedona Church of Light. He usually came from San Diego twice a month to speak to us. He could give a better sermon on Jesus' teachings than many a Baptist minister, and people just couldn't get enough of his talks.

On these special Sundays, people started arriving early, some bringing their own chairs or pillows because there never were enough seats. Yet they kept coming. Many sat on the floor until the room was overflowing, and some had to stand outside at the door. Yes, Hirindrah Singh was by far the most popular and colorful of the many who came to that building over the years. Those were exciting and rewarding days in the history of my humble little church.

At one time this young guru — I believe he was in his early forties — said I had some cobwebs along my spine that needed to be removed. I really had no idea what he meant. He was leaving for a lecture tour the next morning and said he should take care of my cobwebs before he left. He performed what I would call etheric work on my back, for as I lay there I felt nothing. He was evidently working a few inches above my body. He departed the following morning with no further comments about what he had accomplished, if anything.

Suddenly I began to remember all sorts of memories from my early life that apparently had been too painful to recall previously. I had sort of pushed them under, and whenever I had tried to recall that part of my life, it was blank. But now, one by one these events began to resurface. At first it was very disturbing, and I was not sure what I was supposed to do with them. I was angry because Hirindrah had not explained what he had done or how I should handle these painful memories.

For nearly two weeks I wrestled with these unhappy memories and went through them one by one, trying to forgive and to send love to the persons involved. I not only remembered dates, but I saw faces I had long forgotten. I lived through some pretty painful things. The only solution I could come up with was to send love and forgiveness.

After taking care of one incident and feeling a great deal of relief, another memory would come and then another, until apparently I had forgiven and cleansed all these negative unholy memories. I often wondered why I had to go through this process alone, with no help and no counseling. I couldn't even talk about it or confide in anyone. However, I did feel that I had accomplished something important, because I now had total recall of these events without any bad emotions or loss of memory.

Looking back at the incident, I have a feeling of gratefulness toward him. I might never have done this without spending hours on a psychiatrist's couch.

Hirindrah still comes back to Sedona from time to time, but gone are the wonderful pink suits and turbans. He now wears traditional Western business suits. What a shame!

The Guru and the Aliens . . .

Last but not least, let me tell you about another young guru who was the best psychic I have ever known. He was known as Solar. He wore a brown monk-type robe, a long beard and long hair, and always leaned on an odd-looking cane. He claimed he was the reincarnation of Moses, and he took this very seriously. Everyone stared at him because his appearance was so unusual. In fact, he looked like a prophet right out of the Bible, and when I went to lunch with him, as I occasionally did, I got some strange looks, too.

He told me a fascinating story of how he came to be the way he was. In his childhood, living on his father's farm, he was contacted by aliens and became accustomed to their visits. When he finished college, with a promising career ahead of him as a psychologist, he was again visited by the aliens. They wanted him to chuck his career and do a job for them. I don't know what they offered, but finally he agreed to turn his back on his chosen life's work and do their bidding. He told me he thought long and hard about this before he decided in favor of the aliens.

Personally, I thought he had made a huge mistake because it changed his whole life, but who is to say? Perhaps this *was* his life's work, and perhaps he had agreed to do this before this incarnation.

He was firmly dedicated to his association with the aliens. They equipped him with an implant in one ear through which they could contact him. Because of this he became an excellent psychic, one of the best of that time. If he said something would happen, it usually did. He also knew when and where there would be a "saucer" sighting.

I was intrigued by this strange young man, and we became good friends. At times he would stop by my office if I weren't busy, and we would talk for hours. He was reticent to let anyone know what he actually was doing, but gradually over the years I learned his story.

He opened a small metaphysical bookstore in the old uptown area, which at that time was our only business district. This was the first attempt anyone had made to establish a metaphysical bookstore in Sedona, and it was *not* well received or used by the locals. So the shop went through several very lean years.

I believed in what he was trying to do with his shop and wanted to help him, so I lent him $5000. Eventually the shop failed and I lost my money. He gave me all his books, stationery and other things to compensate my loss, but I never did retrieve my loan. At least he tried, and so did I, to make his shop a success.

He seemed to live another mysterious life with several young women who kept out of sight. At that time I could not quite understand what, if anything, was going on.

In those days the old Keller Building was a busy place with lectures, church meetings, seminars, channelings and so on. Around ten o'clock, after the activities of the evening were over, Solar would often stop by my office. "Want to see some flying saucers?" he would ask. And of course I did.

So we would get in my car and drive out to the **Chapel of the Holy Cross** and sit outside up there on the red rocks, watching the sky. Suddenly he would tell me to look in a certain direction — and there they would be, moving in formations of three or more. They were so high I couldn't see them very well, but they definitely were there, and he always knew just where to look and when. Apparently the aliens would tell him they were coming.

Solar told me that sometimes they would show up at odd times and tell him to go to a certain place, usually an airport, and someone would appear out of nowhere and hand him an envelope with enough money in it to buy tickets to wherever he was supposed to go. He did a lot of worldwide traveling in those days. One day he told me the aliens wanted him to go on a trip to Nepal and India, and this time he asked me to help him buy his ticket to India. I had a gold Krugerrand worth about $500. He needed that amount to take the trip, so I gave him the coin. He said he would pay me back and he did.

Before he left for India, he gathered crystals, which he was to "plant" at various places on the planet, including a sacred lake in Nepal. I never did understand what this was all about, but was definitely interested and very curious. I gave him an amethyst crystal to put in the sacred lake, but I never knew what this was supposed to do. These strange trips went on for several years, but I have never known exactly what happened.

When I went on my trip to India in August 1980, this guru was so excited that he offered to drive me (in my car) down to Phoenix to the airport, where I would catch my plane. This two-hour trip to Phoenix was truly enlightening, for Solar told me everything that would happen to me in India — and he was about 90 percent right!

He also instructed me to look deeply into the eyes of every face I came in contact with. He said I would have some strange and unusual experiences, which he called initiations. He spoke truly, for indeed I encountered several mystical and unexplainable events on that unforgettable journey.

When I returned home after that wonderful trip, I found a large cake on my kitchen table. On top of the cake, written in icing, were the words "Happy End of Karma Day." Solar knew that when I was in India, I would be told that I would be free of karma for the rest of my present lifetime and that I would be given the date of my death. Both these things were indeed told to me. However, I seem to have incurred more karma, because since then a lot of lessons have turned up for me to learn. Later I decided to change the date of my 1988 "demise," and as you can see, I was successful.

Solar was always traveling, and months afterward he came to visit me late one night, bringing several of what I called his harem as well as the girl he wanted to marry. They wanted me to perform their wedding ceremony that very night. I expected to do it in my church, but no, he had been "instructed" to be married at the Chapel of the Holy Cross out on Highway 179.

I did a bit of grumbling about why he chose *me* to do his wedding instead of someone younger. After all, I was in my late seventies at this time. Shaking his head at me, he said, "Who else would do it?" He had a point.

By this time it was eleven o'clock at night, but we drove down to the chapel under the brilliant full moon. We were instructed to climb up on one of the nearby red rock formations where the ceremony was to take place. Guided by one flashlight, our little wedding party climbed to the top of the designated rock. As usual, I was wearing high-heeled shoes and had to be boosted and pulled part of the way. (Had I known I would be climbing up the red rocks, I would have worn more appropriate shoes!)

Once there, we held a rather unorthodox wedding ceremony under the light of the moon, with me reading the ritual by way of a flashlight. Then, while standing in a circle, all of us held hands and said a prayer. It turned out to be a beautiful service.

This marriage lasted for about one year. Then Solar again appeared at my front door with his little entourage and another girl he wanted to marry. In those days I often performed some rather strange weddings without question. It seems that *this* girl and the first wife were close friends, and at this point in their relationship they decided the second girl should become the wife, while the first wife was to remain friends with both.

I was not too sure I understood all this, but it was not my custom to question people's reasons for doing what they thought they had to do. So the wedding took place, but this time I did not have to climb the red rocks in the middle of the night.

Much later these two came back to see me and both of them were in a sad state of affairs, not only totally broke but also very disturbed emotionally. So I put them up in my guest room for the night.

It seems this young man had lost his connection with the aliens. They just pulled the plug, so to speak, and set him adrift. They had removed the implant from his ear, which left him deaf in that ear. Not only that, he was like a lost soul, suddenly afloat with no guidance. It almost ruined him.

By this time I had become quite fond of this young man and was truly sad to see what was happening to such a gifted person. I am afraid I questioned inwardly how those aliens could use him for so many years and then abruptly abandon him. It just didn't seem right. And it *wasn't*, according to *our* standards. Now I have learned that these aliens do not have feelings and emotions as we do, and would have had no idea of the damage they had done to him.

His wife was not doing well, either. She would sit all day in my guest bedroom, refusing to speak or participate in any way. Meanwhile I was buying all the groceries, preparing the meals and working full time at my office while they made no effort to help. After two weeks of this uncomfortable arrangement, I realized I must ask them to leave. At my age, I did not need to take care of two capable young people who were making no effort to take care of themselves. By this time in my life I was not bringing in enough income to support more than myself.

It was an extremely unpleasant end to a long and interesting friendship, and I have always regretted that it ended this way. However, I realized I owed it to myself not to take on problems that belonged to other people. After a lifetime of serving others, I finally came to the realization that now my first commitment had to be for my own welfare and happiness.

PART THREE

Sedona to India with
the Pink Prince

24

Planning for the God-Man Tour

$\mathcal{O}$n 1980, the very popular "Pink Prince" (Hirindrah Singh) planned a trip to India to visit the many holy places, the temples and places of pilgrimage in that ancient land. He called this trip the God-Man Tour. Eight Sedonans, mostly members of my church, went on that thirty-three-day trip, and eighteen more came from San Diego, California.

I had always wanted to go to India, and this was my chance, but I kept putting off getting the required immunizations. The list of diseases I must be vaccinated for was formidable, including malaria and bubonic plague. I never had liked the idea of shots, so I had always avoided them. I just couldn't imagine shooting my body full of all those poisons.

But as the days flew by, my deep need to take this trip became almost obsessive, and two days before the trip started, I rushed to a doctor to get the dreaded but necessary inoculations.

"You should have had these two weeks ago," said the doctor.

"But I have only two days," said I.

"They will make you very sick," he said, shaking his head.

"But I *must* have them," I said in my best don't-give-me-any-trouble kind of voice. I wouldn't and couldn't let anything stop me. I *had* to go! Finally he gave me all the shots — and amazingly enough, I had no difficulty, no reaction at all.

So two days later, I was one of the eight Sedonans to start on that most momentous journey. It turned out to be the tour of a lifetime because we were privileged to go to places tourists seldom visit, to attend special events and to meet many wonderful gurus and holy men — all of which I will tell you about later. We visited many holy places, among them the place where Buddha reached enlightenment under a bodhi tree; Satya Sai Baba's ashram; a shrine in Kashmir Valley, where Jesus is said to have left his physical body; and an ancient temple at 12,000 feet that was more than 10,000 years old and is still in use.

I was the oldest woman on Hirindrah's God-Man Tour of India, and there were a few wagers made as to how long I would last on this unusual and rugged trip. Sometimes we spent the night in really primitive accommodations — with no running water and a "bathroom" that was no more than a hole in the cement floor. There were no restaurants, so our food was transported on the backs of the sturdy Indian porters who also cooked our meals.

These men were incredibly dirty, having no water to

bathe in, so when they prepared our food, I had to look the other way or I would have starved. I made a firm pact with myself, declaring, "As long as it doesn't crawl away, I'll eat it." And I did. I was determined to finish this trip upright. My roommate did not eat and became so weak she couldn't stand alone. I helped her walk, carrying all her luggage as well as my own. Eventually one of the men in our group took pity on me and helped.

Part of the trip was on horseback when we rode into the high Himalayas to the Valley of the Flowers, a place of holy pilgrimage at 12,500 feet. Little did those younger people know that I had been a rugged farm girl and was used to horses and camping out. Actually, I survived the trip better than some of them.

This was in no way an ordinary tour, and many unusual and special things happened because we were traveling with Indian royalty. Besides the Pink Prince, there were two princesses (his sisters) and a maharajah (his brother-in-law), who were with us all the way through the Valley of the Flowers as well as in Srinagar, a city in Kashmir. Doors opened wide for us and the red carpet was spread out, for the royal family was recognized wherever we went. Even though they no longer hold royal status, the peasants still treat them with great reverence and even kiss their feet.

Before British rule, Hirindrah and his extensive family lived in an enormous palace of 500 rooms. Prince Hirindrah and the other princes and princesses were brought up by English governesses and special instructors, who made sure they were well-trained in Christianity as well as other major religions. They made certain they knew Western ways, spoke impeccable English and several other languages. Our Pink Prince must have

Mary Lou visits the Taj Mahal.

been an excellent student, for he was comfortably at home wherever he went.

I wouldn't have missed this God-Man tour for anything. From beginning to end, it was an amazing adventure.

25

Sedona to Bombay
and Onward

*M*y great adventure started when I took off from Sedona, flew to New York and on to London, where I and the rest of the tour group boarded an Air India plane for India. After a twelve-and-a-half-hour flight we landed in Bombay. We had crossed the International Date Line and found ourselves arriving on the same calendar date we left New York.

All of us were excited to be taking this tour, and no doubt each person had different expectations. For me, this adventure was the answer to a lifelong dream, and my secret hope was that I would meet Babaji in the high Himalayas. He is a master who lived on Earth 1000 years ago and is reputed to materialize from time to time. I had heard rumors that sometimes he made his appearance in the Valley of the Flowers, and I felt certain I would see him there. Actually I did not, but I did have many other meetings with teachers, masters, gurus and other highly evolved spiritual beings.

Bombay is a vast city, second in size to Mexico City. It is located on the west coast of India and is a beautiful modern metropolis. But like most large cities in the world, the outskirts were sordid, dirty and congested. To my surprise, a Brahma bull was wandering about in the midst of heavy traffic, being fed lovingly by devotees who worship the cow. Never mind the traffic tie-up. Cows are considered holy.

The very moment I stepped off the plane onto the soil of India, I knew I had come home. This was confirmed later in Bangalore on our way back. India is the only place outside of Sedona where I ever felt I definitely belonged. We flew north to New Delhi for our first night, and as the plane flew over miles of country I noticed that the soil was red, almost the same color as ours here in Sedona.

Just as we were registering at the hotel that night, the lights went out. We had to be led up the stairs and helped with our luggage, since we couldn't see a thing. We were given a roll of toilet paper, an article very hard to come by in India. Facial tissue was unheard-of. We had been told to pack two rolls of toilet paper as well as our own tissue, and we would have been in real trouble if we hadn't done so.

All day I'd been looking forward to a good tub soak to help with jet lag, and in anticipation, I'd brought along a box of baking soda and Epsom salts. I found a tub, but it was so dirty I couldn't even think of cleaning it.

So I had to go to bed without my bath. In fact, I had to go bathless during most of the tour because there simply wasn't another tub anywhere except in Bombay and other large cities with big modern hotels.

The next morning we climbed into a ruin of a bus and clattered twenty miles north to Hardwar. I spent the time sightseeing with my Sedona friends while the others had akashic readings. These readings took so long that we had to stay two nights, but even then, we Sedonans had not had our readings. So we made appointments to have them on our return trip. We continued north another twenty miles on our way to Rishikish, which was to be our first base camp for our trip up into the high Himalayas on our way to the Valley of the Flowers.

Echoes of Sedona Past

26

Ashrams and Holy Men

Twenty miles before we reached Rishikish, we stopped at an ashram in Hardwar. When Prince Hirindrah was a young man of about twenty, he had received much valuable instruction and experience from the holy man of this ashram. He was eager to see him again and to introduce us to his old teacher. This delightful visit was another shining highlight of our trip.

The building was so ancient and dilapidated that there was little of it that could still be used. In India this is normal. Nothing is fixed or repaired, just accepted in whatever condition things are in, always going from bad to worse, and no one seems bothered by this state of affairs. We were ushered into a large room with no furniture except a couch on which the guru would sit. We were asked to sit in a semicircle on the dirt floor.

The holy man, who had long, graying hair and beard, appeared with the usual women disciples on each side.

He sat on the couch and began greeting us in perfect English, an apparently well-educated man. He was eager for news about our country and visited with us in a most cordial way.

He then proceeded to give us his famous open-eye meditation, which Hirindrah had told us about. We waited expectantly, as he seemed to be building up energy within himself while doing mudras (stylized hand and arm movements designed to move energy). Then he started staring intently into the eyes of the person at the end of our line.

I have never encountered such powerful eyes as his when he stared deeply into each person's eyes in turn. When he came to me, my head felt like it had exploded and I came near to swooning. As he came back around for the second time I felt the same jolt, only not as strong. When he returned to the other end of the semi-circle, he concentrated for some time on one of the men in the group. This man did not believe in God and was one of the chief revelers on the trip. The guru seemed to throw his entire strength into his contact with this man, while continuing to do mudras with his hands. I noticed that the guru's entire body was vibrating. The energy built up so strongly that he actually lifted a few inches off the couch. This was the first time I'd seen anyone levitate. After this moving ceremony was over, I noticed that the man had tears running down his face and obviously was quite shaken. He told us he never again would deny there was a God.

Next we left Hardwar for Rishikish, located in the foothills of the Himalayas where the Ganges River pours into the area in a tumultuous roar of swiftly flowing water.

In Rishikish we spent one day touring the deteriorated temples built along the far bank of the Ganges. They stretched for miles as far as the eye could see, all the way between Hardwar and Rishikish. They were very, very old and looked as if they could collapse at any moment, but somehow they held together and were in daily use. We had crossed the holy river, walking over a bridge lined on both sides with pitiful beggars. We were warned not to give them anything or we would be besieged from then on. It was difficult to resist their pleading, but later we learned that beggars make more money than most workers.

We visited an ashram where a guru was being hand-fed by his women disciples. He sat on a couch while the women peeled fruit and actually put it in his mouth. He would have starved otherwise, because food no longer interested him — he had given up the world. At first he adamantly refused to allow us to come into his presence, but finally, after some coaxing from our royalty, he most reluctantly allowed us entrance but refused to speak to us. Apparently he sensed that all of us were not on a spiritual journey, and some of the actions going on among part of our group was not to his liking. He just sat there glaring angrily at us.

We were each given a slice of apple, which is a custom in ashrams, when the guru suddenly cut loose and in the Hindu language gave us a very heated lecture. Of course we didn't understand a word, but his disapproval of us was more than abundantly obvious. Fortunately, some of the other ashrams and temples received us more graciously.

Because there was no bridge, we had to take a ferry to get back to the other side of the river. This experience was pretty tense for me. The ferry was crowded with natives and everyone stood, body to body. There was no railing on the sides of the deck, and I have no idea why people didn't fall into the river. I was fortunate to have a stationary pole to cling to, but it didn't do much to calm my quivering nerves.

27

Valley of the Flowers
and Sikh Warriors

The next day our group climbed into what must have been the most dilapidated bus in the world, departed Rishikish and started the arduous trip up the mountain. This pilgrimage to the legendary Valley of the Flowers was one of the highlights of my life. Many believe that ancient Great Ones have lived here for thousands of years and still do.

We rattled and creaked our way upward through the beautiful and wild forest country. Because we were traveling with royalty (a prince, two princesses and a maharajah), we were able to pass through areas tourists seldom have access to. There were security checks along the route because of China's invasion of Tibet, and at times we were very close to the Tibetan border.

I shall never forget that bus trip. We drove on narrow, one-way dirt roads that were open only at certain hours of the day, depending on whether one was going up the mountain or down. The Indian bus drivers were pretty wild, recklessly careening around curves of the mountain road — which frequently had a 2000- to 3000-foot drop over the side! From our position we looked out upon vast, straight-up-and-down mountain country, but few of us were concentrating on the spectacular view. Needless to say, there was much screaming by some of the female passengers. I tried to convince them we were in no trouble because we all had too much karma to work out. I don't think my words were particularly reassuring.

I remember one spot where we drove right under a giant waterfall, which crashed over our heads as we passed under it. After an all-day drive we stopped at a small mountain village to spend the night and we were taken to a cement building with a cement floor and little cubicles with cots on which we slept. Our sleeping bags were our most precious possessions; without them we would have had to sleep between very old and dirty woolen blankets. Water (and what I would laughingly refer to as a restroom) was outside.

While our kitchen crew (who also carried our luggage and food) prepared a meal for us out in the open beside the building, we went for a stroll up the one street, where a few ancient buildings stood. We were greeted by the sight of a group of people who lined the street to watch us walk by. We felt like aliens from another planet. They were more curious about us than we were about them, for they seldom saw people from our part of the world. One young woman reached out to touch my hair and feel my clothes.

The next morning, after a quick meal that did not resemble any breakfast I had ever eaten, we got back on the bus and rumbled on our way. We came to the end of the road before noon and again had a repast that resembled nothing I had ever eaten. Almost everything was loaded with curry — even the morning meal — which disguised whatever else it was or what was wrong with it. This was really a great opportunity to test how flexible we could be, since at this phase of the trip there obviously was no turning back.

At one point we walked through a heavily guarded gate. I innocently took a picture of it, then all hell broke loose! My camera was taken away from me and I was looked upon with great suspicion until Prince Hirindrah came to my rescue. Beyond the gate our horses were waiting for us, so we mounted and in a drizzling rain headed up the mountain to the Valley of the Flowers. One ignorant soul opened her umbrella, which almost caused her horse to plunge over the edge of the steep trail. We had rain capes that sort of protected us, but they were not really adequate.

The trip was fantastically beautiful if you were not being overly concerned with your comfort. We met occasional pilgrims who were either coming down the trail or going up to the Valley of the Flowers. They were very friendly and called out a traditional greeting, except for a wealthy Sikh woman who was making the trip in a large basket on the back of a scrawny but muscular young man. When he stopped to rest along the trail, we took their picture, which she seemed to resent, for she covered her face.

Finally we reached the place where we were to spend the next two nights, a government rest house built during British rule. All we had for a shower was a bucket of cold water to pour over us. The toilet, of course, was the standard hole in the floor. We slept on cots in one

Woman being carried to the Valley of the Flowers in a basket.

large room and were fairly comfortable except for the 10,000-foot altitude, which gave many of us severe headaches.

Only then, with my head pounding, did I remember the advice I had been given by Solar, the young Sedona guru who had driven me to the Phoenix airport: "Be sure to take plenty of aspirin with you." I had never taken aspirin in all my life and had seen no reason to start now. But here in this high altitude I dearly wished I had taken his words seriously. One of my tour friends offered aspirin, which I gratefully swallowed before I was able to sleep.

The next morning we gathered around a large campfire for the morning meal, then mounted our horses for the last part of the trip to the Valley of the Flowers, another climb of 2500 feet. This was an unbelievably beautiful sight! The trees at this altitude were huge, al-

The Pink Prince with his sister, Princess Diamond.

most like giant redwoods, and the rhododendrons were as high as trees. Snow-covered mountains at the end of the valley towered about 10,000 feet above us. Although it was the end of September, a few flowers were still in blossom, and we were told that in late summer there were over a thousand different flower species blooming here. Words fail to describe the beauty of this valley, but the experience was well worth the effort to get there.

Lunchtime came. The sun was warm and felt wonderful as we sat on blankets provided for us. While we ate our lunch a very tiny Indian holy man came to join us. He spoke a little English, and when we asked him where he was from, he replied that the world was his home. He told us he had known we were coming and that he would join us for lunch. While we were eating, he gave us a long, interesting discourse in his own language, which was interpreted for us by Hirindrah.

While we were there a young man came down the mountain leading a beautiful little lamb, which we admired and petted. Later we found out that this lamb was served to us for dinner that night.

At this high altitude I had trouble getting my breath, and my gasping and choking frightened my friends. Everyone insisted I go back to our camp at the rest house on the 10,000-foot level. I was terribly disappointed that I had to leave, feeling that if I were destined to die at this time, there could be no more fitting a place than here. Being an asthmatic, I knew I was crowding my luck to breathe at all at that altitude. It had occurred to me that it would be interesting indeed to see if I could survive there. I was also certain I could keep on going until I found Babaji. However, I went down to camp and the rest of the group came back a few hours later.

That evening we were invited to a Sikh temple, where it just happened that the most famous spiritual singer in all India, who also was making a pilgrimage, would sing. We gathered in the primitive temple and sat upon the ground in a semicircle. The head Sikh holy man opened a huge holy book that lay on a golden stand framed in gaudy Christmas decorations and proceeded to read the lesson for the evening. The Sikhs do not believe in a God of form. To them God is formless, and they do not worship idols. This is just the opposite of the Hindu religion, in which many gods and numerous idols are worshiped, including Jesus.

The great singer was a handsome old man with a white, wavy beard extending to his waist. He accompanied himself with a small hand-held organ that operated somewhat like an accordion. It was quite a treat and an honor to be invited there.

In the midst of the singing one of the girls in our tour

group let out a piercing shriek, loudly accusing a Hindu sitting behind her of molestation. What followed was more exciting than anything I had ever seen on television. The Sikhs are the warrior class of India and carry large spears, a dagger in their turbans and sharp things on their wrists and hands that look like very lethal weapons (like brass knuckles). They leapt to

A Sikh warrior in a peaceful mood.

their feet, spears drawn, and the native women rushed forward, covering the guilty man with their bodies. They knew that if blood were drawn, the hapless man would be killed.

Hirindrah, his sister and the holy man tried to reason with the angry Sikhs, but molesting a woman, especially in a Sikh temple, was like committing instant suicide. Because the accused man was a Hindu, it made matters even worse, for he was not really welcome there.

After much angry talk, he was taken to our campsite,

where a large campfire lit up the blackness of the night with eerie shadows. That scene is etched in my memory forever: the Hindu, with his hands tied behind his back, being shoved ahead by the warriors shouting that he was now to die; the princess making an impassioned plea for the Hindu's life; and Prince Hirindrah speaking about compassion. But the Sikh warriors were not listening. Already they had drawn their own blood, as was their custom before killing.

Hirindrah, himself a Sikh, reminded the warriors that according to their holy book, they must let the Hindu go if he kissed the woman's feet and asked her forgiveness. Apparently, Hirindrah knew the holy law because, reluctantly, the Sikh warriors agreed. However, the accused man screamed in terror and struggled to get away. The worst thing that could happen to a man of his religion was to kiss a woman's feet. But when the warriors leaped forward with their spears drawn, he quickly changed his mind, kissed the woman's feet and asked her forgiveness. I regret to say that she gave it quite ungraciously.

There was much angry muttering among the Sikh warriors, but according to their law, they had to let him go. The terrified man quickly disappeared into the dark night. Later I heard that he would indeed be lucky if he got out of the vicinity alive.

The princess was very angry with the girl who had caused the incident and gave her a stern lecture about making such a big thing of it, nearly causing a man to lose his life. Several other women in our group said that the same man had touched them or tried to fondle them, but they had just given him a dirty look and moved out of reach. They hadn't made a production of the event.

166

The next morning we arose to find several giant Sikh warriors standing around our campfire, dressed in brilliant blue clothing and turbans trimmed with a silver symbol such as a star or a moon. Their swords were in their hands and their daggers were stuck into their turbans. We found all this pretty frightening. But they seemed friendly, just very curious, not used to seeing people like us. I snapped a picture of them in the early dawn, but it didn't come out well.

This event probably was one of the most exciting parts of our trip.

28

Healing Ritual and Unexplained Events

*W*e set out early the next morning for Badrinath, a city at 12,000 feet near the Tibetan border. We wanted to see an ancient temple said to have been in continuous use for over 10,000 years. This was another scary trip by bus on winding, narrow roads. We arrived in the afternoon and were shown to our quarters, another government rest house with the usual sparse facilities.

We were travel-weary, but we wanted to see the temple, which was high on the side of a mountain overlooking the small town of Badrinath. We proceeded down the mountain to a bridge over a wild, rushing river — one of the two that merge to form the Ganges.

We climbed up the hill on the other side to the bathhouses, where hot mineral springs came gushing out of the mountain. There were separate bathhouses for men and women. We were to immerse ourselves in the warm pool before we would be allowed into the temple. We took off our shoes and left them at the foot of the 300 steps leading up to the temple. I was barely able to breathe at this altitude. I think it was willpower and determination that led me up those seemingly endless steps.

At the top we entered a walled compound, which was like a small village with souvenir shops for visitors. This was a shock to me. I don't know what I expected, but certainly not souvenir shops. As we entered the crowded temple and pressed forward through the crowd, we came to a sunken area in which a team of holy men were doing a healing ritual with chanting, bells and gongs. The din was almost overwhelming. It seemed that we were expected, because we were told to wait and that we were next.

After what seemed a very long time, the sound subsided and we were brought forward to stand at the edge of the pit. As we were receiving our noisy healing ritual, we noticed some steps leading upward beyond a gated area. A robed person, obviously very important, came down the stairs to an area below where a great, green stone stood. This stone was called a lingam. The next day we found out that this personage was the greatest holy man in India and that he would invite us to his dwelling place on another level below the temple.

When our ritual was finished, we were told to leave by the side entrance. People lined both sides of the narrow hall, so we had to go single file. I had never seen such a mixture of all kinds of people in strange native attire. There were people from Tibet (we were only a few miles from the Chinese-Tibetan border, which was heavily guarded), and there were several women with long gold earrings that hung down to their shoulders and a matching one swinging from their noses. I felt we were truly in a foreign land; the atmosphere was definitely strange and exotic. As we proceeded down the hall, I remembered Solar's words to me: "Be sure to look deeply into the eyes of every face." So I looked into every face as we walked. Those faces were fascinating.

We passed a monk dressed in a hooded brown robe, who stared at each person passing as if he were searching for someone. When our eyes met he became very excited, as though I was the one he'd been watching for. I can't explain how I sensed this, but I stopped and gave him the Indian gesture of hands together to the forehead, which means "the God in me greets the God in you." He broke into a great smile and began a lengthy prayer or discourse, which astounded me. I could not understand what he was telling me. I wish I knew. When he finished, I mumbled, "May God bless you," for lack of something to say, and stumbled on. When I later asked, not one of our group had observed this happening. Apparently no one was held up when I stopped, because not one person behind or ahead of me remembered any delay.

It was already dark when we left the temple and started down the mountain. As we began our descent, someone came to give us an invitation from a holy woman who was also there on a pilgrimage to the temple. Being aware of our presence, she had asked that we come to her quarters. She was a silent guru and often went for months without speaking. But wonder of wonders, she not only spoke to us, but she did so in English, greeting us warmly. She gave each of us a blessing, a great honor bestowed on us by this special lady in white. She also allowed us to touch her — very unusual in India.

Later we went on down the mountain, crossed the bridge and started up the other side toward our quarters. At this point I was so weary from the long day and the altitude (which was causing me to breathe laboriously) that I became faint and started to stagger. It was dark, so no one noticed, each intent on his own journey up the mountain.

Then out of the darkness came a young Indian man who took my arm and said in English, "Mother, may I help you?" In India, age is revered, and if you have white hair you are treated with much respect. Gratefully I accepted his assistance. I don't know how I could ever have made it without him. When we neared the government rest house, I reached into my purse to give him a tip, but when I looked up he had vanished completely out of sight, as if he had melted into thin air. This was most unusual, because Indians always accept tips from travelers. By this time I began to think maybe I was hallucinating, especially when the next day I could not find anyone who had observed this young man helping me. Could it have been the rarified atmosphere?

The next morning we were taken to visit another famous guru who was said to be over 200 years old. He was sitting against a beautiful moss-covered boulder in the morning sun, wearing nothing but a loincloth. He was a genial old man with long hair and a beard, and his eyes were keenly alert. He spoke to us in his own language, interpreted by Hirindrah. I treasure a photo I took of him.

Then we were invited to visit the great holy man of the temple, whom we had seen the evening before when he had been descending the steps behind the altar. His abode was about halfway up the other side of the mountain. This visit was another moment to cherish in my

A 200-year-old guru in Badrinath.

necklace of memories of sacred India. He gave each of
us a little token — a blessing to carry with us.

29

Houseboats in Kashmir

*W*e Sedonans were truly in search of spiritual experiences, but as the God-Man Tour progressed, we realized that the group from California was traveling for different reasons. It became apparent that those of us from Sedona and four others were the only ones on a spiritual quest. The rest of the group were obviously on a quest for bed partners. As time went on, we began to call our tour "the Sodom and Gomorrah trip."

Our next destination was Srinagar in Kashmir, a beautiful mountain valley at about 6500 feet. Srinagar has always been known as "the Jewel of India." (At the present time, India and Pakistan are once again on the verge of fighting over ownership of Kashmir.) We went there by bus. We were to stay on houseboats on scenic Lake Dal and have a much-needed rest after our rugged journey of the last few days.

The houseboats were absolutely luxurious, beautifully furnished with hand-carved furniture and splendid draperies. To move about the lake, we had to summon water taxis, small boats that held only four people each. We did a lot of exploring and saw floating islands covered with flowers, as well as other little boats manned by the wily, floating entrepreneurs who were eager to sell their wares. They offered lovely handwoven and decorated wool shawls, carved sandalwood statues and other treasures. These fellows would come rowing alongside our boat and begin their "pitch and show."

I bought a couple of shawls and a sandalwood Buddha to take home — I still have them. A few minutes after I made my purchase, the same little boat came alongside again and the young man who had sold the items to me thrust a handful of money at me, saying he had taken advantage of me and charged way too much. I tried to hand it back to him, but he refused, saying that I reminded him of his white-haired mother, and he would not like to think someone would take advantage of her. Later all of us had a good laugh over this, and I remarked that it was wonderful to see what white hair could do for you in India.

One morning a couple of Tibetan refugees arrived and set out their wares on our "front porch." Some of the articles were very old and unique, quite different from anything we had seen in any of the shops. I spotted an ancient temple bell and picked it up and rang it. Much to my embarrassment, big tears began to run down my face. I put the bell down and ran to my room. I was having a good cry when it suddenly occurred to me that someone might buy *my* bell. Quickly I dried my face and rushed out to the porch.

As I reached for the bell someone else was reaching for it. But I was faster. I grabbed it, saying, "Sorry, this is *my* bell." That bell had tapped into some ancient life in my past when I was probably a monk and rang a bell just like this one. It surely did shake me up.

While on the houseboats we observed that our cook and servers washed everything in the lake off the back porch — dishes, silverware, towels and sheets. Our meals were served elegantly with fine china and silver, flowers on the table and wonderful food. This was a real treat after what we had just experienced. However, before our stay was over, we all came down with a very bad case of vomiting and diarrhea. As we were leaving, we met a man on shore who told us (in English) that Lake Dhal was a giant sewer. He remarked that every bit of sewage from Srinagar and the surrounding country emptied into that lake. No wonder we were ill.

Nevertheless., I shall never forget the beauty of the Kashmir valley. We had some wonderful side tours while there, one to an ancient shrine where Jesus was said to be entombed in a very interesting big hand-carved casket. The Indian people firmly believe, from their old records, that Jesus finished his life there, living to a great old age. Everywhere we went in India, statues of Jesus were always standing among their many gods. Apparently he was greatly revered and considered a part of their ancient history. When I was in Greece many years ago I saw the same thing. Wherever there were statues of Greek gods, among them was also a statue of Jesus.

You seldom hear of it, but there are many Christians in India. We visited one Christian church, built on a high hill up another 300 steps, which was established by St. Thomas. He had spent the last part of his life there and built the church on that hill. Later another church was built on the same spot.

Before we left Kashmir we took a daylong trip to Gulmarg, right on the border of Afghanistan, where there was a magnificent golf course at 9500 feet — the highest golf course in the world. It was very green and surrounded by forest. On the highest point was a club-house, not very fancy, but adequate. We had lunch in the dining room. Some of the party took horseback trips, but the rest of us sat on top of that mountain where the air was so clear you could see into forever. Kashmir is the northernmost part of India and the panorama from there was really out of this world.

After our weeklong stay in Srinagar, we flew back to New Delhi (on another plane held together with barbed wire and chewing gum). Here we prepared for the final leg of our trip, a five-day visit at Satya Sai Baba's ashram.

30

Sai Baba's Ashram

Going south on the way back, our last adventure was to be in Bangalore, a very modern city, which was surprisingly clean. Bangalore is in the southern part of India halfway between the east and west coasts, and it has an ideal year-round climate. It is where Satya Sai Baba has his ashram, just outside the city. But after we checked into our hotel, we found that Sai Baba was not there but was farther north in his other ashram in Puttaparthi.

The night we checked into our hotel the lights went out before we got to our rooms, and we had to find our way up the stairs in the dark with the help of a hotel employee. There was pandemonium for a while, but by the time we had climbed several flights of stairs, the lights came back on. We had already learned that this is a frequent occurrence in India. Some small towns regularly shut off the electricity at nine in the evening.

The next morning we chartered a bus to take us the

150 miles north to the other ashram in Puttaparthi. This was another of those feeble old vehicles we were becoming accustomed to. Well, that poor bus took five hours to cover those miles, on what eventually became a very primitive dirt road full of ruts and holes. We passed through a few small villages on the way. Obviously they had no school buildings, because we often saw a group of children sitting under a large tree with their teacher. The only water was the town pump where everyone came with water vessels. We actually saw some people taking showers under the pump.

These people, who in our estimation were shockingly poor, were all friendly and smiling. They seemed to be as happy as children at play, apparently not even realizing their poverty. How can you miss something you never had and do not even know exists?

We arrived in the small village of Puttaparthi late in the afternoon. At the edge of the town we were amazed to see a truly magnificent temple and grounds. We were astonished to learn it was Sai Baba's ashram — standing in splendor in the midst of this poverty-stricken wilderness. The gate at the entrance was a large, highly decorated monument in itself, and we walked down an avenue lined with palms, behind which were ornamental walls. The light-blue temple at the end of the tree-lined street was gorgeous, decorated with angels and carved Indian deities painted in pink and yellow. As I took in this amazing spectacle, I had the fleeting feeling that it was India's version of Disneyland. It was almost too much decoration and paint.

I must at this point say that I was not overly thrilled to be in Sai Baba's ashram. Years before, when I first saw a picture of him, I had shuddered and disliked him intensely, which was rather unusual for me. (This is the

Sai Baba's ashram in Puttaparthi.

crux of this story, as you will later see.)

We were there for five days. The eight of us from Sedona were assigned our quarters, which consisted of a small room with a cement floor barely big enough for our sleeping bags. The room was bare except for a large picture of Sai Baba. The open window was barred to keep out the monkeys, which abound everywhere in India. We were warned not to put anything along the windowsill because the monkeys would reach in and take it. One of the girls forgot and left her toothpaste there. A monkey grabbed it and squeezed it dry.

Our "bathroom" was a small cubicle containing a knee-high water pipe and faucet, and a hole in the floor with a bucket beside it. The bars kept out the monkeys but did nothing for the very large mosquitoes that buzzed us all night. We slept with our heads inside our sleeping bags. I was unimpressed with the whole scenario.

The food was palatable but certainly not gourmet. Breakfast consisted of rice patties with curry sauce and coffee that was half coffee and half milk with lots of sugar — ugh! My roommate was still steadfastly refusing to eat and was so weak I had to hold her up. We found fruit outside the gate and freshly squeezed juices that helped sustain us.

After breakfast everyone would gather in the compound in front of the temple, sitting on the ground in

Mary Lou wearing a sari.

the hot sun and fighting off flies while they awaited his highness. Western wear was not permitted in the ashram, so we women wore saris, which are typical Indian women's attire. If we felt overcome with the heat and started to loosen our sari at the neckline, an ashram woman would come and jerk it back and give us an angry look. Men and women were kept apart in different areas of the ashram — even married people — so the three couples in our group had been separated.

After about two hours of sitting, we were rewarded by the sight of Sai Baba, who appeared wearing a flame-colored gown with a train. He strolled along the lane in front of the gathered crowd, greeted some of them, took notes from a few (refusing to take others) and gave the crowd his blessings, after which he went back into the temple.

At this point I remarked rather irreverently, "The show's over for today, folks. Let's go home." My words elicited a few angry stares. I pulled myself together and prepared to endure the experience, because there was no way I could get out of there until five days later, when the bus would come and retrieve us. I tried to suffer through all this with as much grace as I could muster.

Prince Hirindrah and his two sisters were still with us, all of them devotees of Sai Baba. About the second day we were unexpectedly invited for a private audience with Sai Baba, probably because of the royalty with us. The people of the ashram considered this highly un-usual, because he had not granted an audience to any-one for three months. Our audience with Sai Baba alienated us from them even more, and the women ac-tually spit at us and gathered stones as though they were about to throw them at us. This further deepened our anxiety to get out of there. (I am sure Sai Baba had nothing to do with these actions, but surely he must have been aware of the jealousy that was being played out among his devotees.)

He invited us into a large room. With us were two young women from San Diego who had been his follow-ers for some time. During the trip they had proudly told us how Sai Baba had come to them in their meditations and given them instructions. They spoke up and thanked him for appearing and for his wisdom. He replied, "That was not I who appeared to you. It was either your fantasy or an astral being posing as me."

We were all stunned by his declaration. Needless to say, the young women were very upset, and he lost a couple of followers right then. Looking at each one of us in the room, he said, "I am not your guru. Go within. Your guru is within."

I was amazed that he knew this truth, because he allowed his own people to worship him as God and kiss his feet. Then I remembered that many people need to have a living person to worship, apparently not yet able to grasp the idea that God is within.

Sai Baba did some materializations, handing various people a locket, a ring, a medal or vibhuti (a type of sacred ash). One of Hirindrah's sisters spoke to him in his language and sounded very angry. They had a heated discussion. Sai Baba may have lost more disciples at this point, because the following day the Pink Prince and his sisters were as anxious to leave as we were.

After this meeting, ashram life became more unbearable. We spent a lot of time outside the grounds in the small village, exploring and eating in little open-air eating places. We tried to see some sign of the riches and opulence of the ashram in this village, but none was visible.

On the fifth day we could hardly wait for our bus, and we sat outside waiting for it to arrive. When it finally showed up, we cheered and laughed with relief. But this is not the end of the story, because what happened the next day was indeed a shock to me.

31

Akashic Reading

The next morning six of us went for our readings at the ashram in Bangalore where the Akashic Records had been kept for 6000 years. These records are recorded in tiny Sanskrit letters on the inner side of a palm frond. The rest of our group went on to Bombay and we were to meet them there that evening.

Our readings took up most of that day. While waiting, we sat in a small room where we were served tea and bananas. At the end of the day, after my twelfth banana, I was sure I never could eat another one, but no other food was available.

My reading was first and was delayed for an hour. (Years later I found out there was a very special reason for the delay.) Finally my name was called, and I was introduced to the old saint, who was keeper of the ashram, and to my interpreter, a Brahmin with white hair and golden eyes. I had never seen eyes like his. He was very light-skinned, tall, slender, well-educated and spoke perfect English.

The old saint gave me an amazingly accurate summary of my life, which was 99 percent correct. It was certainly impressive, but the rest of the information I was to be given that day was so astounding that it left me almost speechless.

He kept saying what a difficult life I had led. At one point, remembering how hard it had been, tears came running down my face. When I looked at the interpreter, I saw that he also was crying. I asked why he wept and he said, "I know this is your first trip to India. I have never visited your country, but you and I are old friends. Your joy is my joy and your sorrow, my sorrow." I was deeply touched because all through the reading, if I laughed, he laughed, and when I cried, he cried.

I was also told about one of my former lives in India when I was a disciple of Shirdi Baba, who in this present lifetime is Sai Baba. And I was told about my present life from that day forward to my death in 1988. I was even told that I would not die in a hospital, but would just go into samadhi (deep meditation) and leave my body.

All at once the two men looked at each other and said that Sai Baba was present. Of course I could not see him, but obviously they could. They remarked that he never came to their readings, but now he was here asking that they get *his* records out of the Hall of Records. So they were sent in, wrapped in red cloth. The old saint tried to hand this package to me, but I pulled back, refusing to touch it. They tried to tell me it was important, but I kept refusing. After a while their insistence finally got to me, so I took it and was told to hold it to my forehead. When I did this, they said, "You have now been released from the curse of the guru."

I was truly shocked as I listened to them tell me that when Shirdi Baba had been my guru in my last life, he had cursed me and had me stoned to death for some infraction of his rules. At that time I had been the same age I was at this very day and hour. This was the reason for the delay in my reading. They had waited for the time to coincide with the hour of my curse. Shirdi Baba's curse had made me come back to Earth to live this very difficult lifetime. In my previous life, I had apparently reached the point when I was through with the Earth plane and would not have to reincarnate again — except for the curse.

In a daze and feeling almost total disbelief in the whole episode, I went back to the room where the others were waiting their turn.

Late that afternoon we departed by plane to meet the rest of our group in Bombay. There we were put up in a Hari Krishna temple, which was really impressive with its gold ceilings and fountains. However, it had third-rate accommodations for visitors. That night I tossed and turned before I finally went to sleep. I awoke with a start at 2:30 and sat straight up in bed with the feeling that a mountain had been lifted off my head and a sensation I had never experienced before nor since. It was like a release and a rapture that I can even now recall. I knew then that the curse must have been true. However, I still could not forgive Sai Baba for what he had done to me in his past life when he was Shirdi Baba.

When I returned home to Sedona I searched for months for a book about the life of Shirdi Baba. I finally found one. I spent the next few months reading that book. It was a slow process because I was living that past life over and over again. It was all so familiar and so very traumatic. By the time I finished the book,

I was able to forgive Sai Baba for what he had done. But I still wondered how a guru could treat a disciple in that manner.

Now, almost twenty years later, I have gained the wisdom to see that he may have done me a service in making me come back for another lifetime at such an auspicious time for Earth. I can see how much I have learned and gained this time, polishing a few more facets. And how wonderful to be able to experience this special time of emergence into light! My curse has turned into my blessing.

My feelings for Sai Baba have been healed. He may have loved me so much that he was giving me another life with another chance to grow and learn. I may never know. Surprisingly, there is even more to this story.

32

Keeper of the Records
Visits Sedona

ave you ever had a tarot reader or a psychic tell you that you would leave this Earth plane at such-and-such an age or name a specific date for your demise? If so, you know that, try as you may to put the time out of your mind, it is stuck on a subconscious level and will come popping up to haunt you. This is what happened to me. I carried this information around with me for several years, noting occasionally that I had eight years left, then seven years and then six.

One day that year I answered the ring of my doorbell and, much to my total amazement, there stood the son of the old Indian saint who had been the keeper of the Akashic Records in Bangalore. The elderly father had passed on and the son, who had been trained from birth to take over his father's place, was now the keeper of the records.

He had been lecturing and touring in the United States, and when he was in Tucson he told his friends that he must go to Sedona to see Mary Lou Keller. So here he was at my door, having been driven by some of his tour group. They dropped him off for several hours, and I had this unexpected chance to enjoy his delightful company.

I put him on my patio and brought him a cup of coffee prepared the way they like it in India, half milk and sugar. He said it was the best coffee he had tasted in the States. He was able to see the many devas and nature spirits in my wooded place (my joyful jungle on Keller Lane off Upper Red Rock Loop Road) and was having such a great time that he almost forgot why he had come.

He had brought my Akashic Records with him all the way from India, saying he had to correct something that had been told me at my 1980 reading in Bangalore. He explained that the given date of my death (1988) was not an absolute. If when that time came I had a new project to take on, a new interest and reason for living, I could extend my life four more years. At the end of that first extension, if my enthusiasm for life was still strong, I could extend it another four years and so on. This opened up a whole new realization for me. I learned that a date with death is not a certainty. It depends on one's motivation to live, one's enthusiasm and attitude toward life.

However, in March 1988, my health hit an all-time low and my date with death was fast approaching. I was really tired and weary of the whole effort just to stay alive and maintain myself, and I couldn't think of one good reason to stick around. I was doing an excellent job of meeting my deadline.

Shortly before this I had attended several of the Atlanto channelings through Arthur Fanning, and suddenly one day I decided to have a private reading. Weak and wobbly, I made the effort to pull myself together and drive to Cornville for my appointment. The first thing I asked was, "Is there any good reason why I have to stay in this body? It's just not cooperating with me." He laughed and laughed and said that indeed there was a good reason — and proceeded to change my whole attitude. He pointed out how exciting life could be and said that I had a lot more to do, and I must get on with it. Arthur Fanning has published many articles and books. He continues to give readings, hold weekend seminars and channel. He was a wonderful teacher to me at a time when I really needed encouragement.

The hour I spent with him changed the entire course of my life. It turned my head around, and as I drove home I made the decision to pull myself up by the bootstraps and live. This was a momentous decision, because with the meditation techniques he gave me, I began to get well. A year later my friends were saying, "What are you doing? You look ten years younger."

The essential point of this story is: If you want to live, no matter what is going on in your life, including your state of health, you can make the decision to change your attitude about living. Begin to enjoy the many simple things all around you that are so often taken for granted. Watch for the little miracles that happen every day, acknowledge them and say "thank-you" for the gift of life, which is so very precious. Greet every new morning with joy and gratitude for being allowed to live in a body at this very special time in history. Learn to love your body and treat it like your favorite pet.

If you can do this, those cut-off dates will haunt you no more because you are living life with a courageous and victorious heart.

PART FOUR

Reflections

33

Instant Karma

*I*nstant karma can be presented to you no matter where you live; however, it seems to happen more often in Sedona. Lessons appear to catch up with you much faster here than anywhere else. I heard about this odd phenomenon soon after moving to this red rock country. Mention was often made by friends in the know about such things, that instant karma was a frequent happening in Sedona. This fact really didn't make much of an impact on me until the day it caught up with me in a matter of just two hours.

In the 1950s, the business activity centered in uptown Sedona near the intersection of highways 89A and 179. To tell the truth, there was very little business to keep us fully occupied, so around ten in the morning everyone converged on the few small coffee shops to chat and gossip. I must admit that gossip was one of our favorite pastimes, since there wasn't much else to do.

One morning a friend and I walked into the Ranch

Kitchen and found the shop crowded and buzzing with conversation. As we made for the only available seats at the counter, we observed a mutual friend (also a businesswoman) sitting in the far corner having a cup of coffee with a fellow we considered a disreputable character. He was well-known for his habit of preying on elderly and lonely widows. With his charming ways, he persuaded many a widow to part with her money.

I said to my friend, "How could Sue (not her name) possibly be seen in public with that despicable man? If she has some kind of business with him, she should do it behind closed doors where no one can see her." I grumbled and rambled on and on over our coffee and then went back to my office.

Two hours later I sauntered across the street to have lunch at the **Turtle** (later called **The Orchards**). It was a popular place to have lunch, and I walked in and found there was only one booth left. I sat down and ordered a bowl of soup.

Just as my soup arrived, I saw this same man (whom I would not have been caught dead with) come into the restaurant and glance around the room. Seeing no empty table and me occupying a booth all by myself, he walked over and sat down. Much to my horror, he said, "I hope you don't mind sharing your space." What could I say? I gulped down my soup and ran out like a scared rabbit, realizing that most of the local people lunching there knew me. They couldn't help but see me sitting in the booth alone with this "despicable character" and probably were doing some fancy speculating of their own.

I also knew that I had just experienced the much-discussed "instant karma." I had been put into the exact situation that I had seen Sue experience just two hours before when I had rushed to judgment.

Needless to say, I learned a valuable lesson. Whenever I am tempted to pass judgment or wonder what certain people are doing out together, I quickly remind myself that circumstances may not be what they appear to be, and after all, it is none of my business.

Echoes of Sedona Past

34

Fear and Anger

Many friends have come and gone during my Sedona sojourn. Some moved to greener pastures. Some left this mortal life to move on into another dimension. Two of my very dear friends left much too soon, in my estimation. This took place at least thirty years ago. One was about my age and the other was ten years younger. I have spent a lot of time pondering over what caused their early demise, other than the fact that we all have our cut-off time. It certainly was not their eating habits. Both were strict vegetarians and were extremely concerned about what went into their bodies. Yet they both passed on from cancer.

Dory was a delightful little person, cheerful and loving. In fact, you always came away from a visit with her feeling a sense of self-worth because she saw only the best in everyone, be they a friend or total stranger. I felt she was a living saint. Still, probing amongst my memories of her life, I began to unearth something that didn't fit with the rest of what I knew about her. Dory listened to all of the doom-and-gloom soothsayers and began hoarding food and water, and she even had a couple of guns. She seldom spoke about fears of what she thought was coming in the near future, but it was quite obvious that she was preparing to survive and to defend herself.

Could this be the answer to my question? Had this lovely pure spirit allowed fear of the future to creep into her consciousness until it began to eat at her internally? I often grieved over her passing, thinking it was so unfair for her to contact a terminal disease. But was it?

Betty was also a positive metaphysical thinker, involved in many interesting projects and studies and seemingly in vigorous health. I searched through my memory bank, wondering what went wrong. I finally had a clue. She was extremely angry with the United States government and bureaucrats, and she read everything she could find on the workings of the underground forces trying to take over the world. I also noticed that she was excessively angry with her family and fairly seethed when she mentioned them. Here again was the answer — a deep, constant anger that was eating at her inwardly, upsetting the harmony and balance in her physical body.

These contemplations have convinced me of the value of our attitudes, not only those we show the world, but the abiding fears and angers we may entertain secretly within ourselves. Nothing in the material world should be so important that we allow it to cause such fear or anger.

Our real peace and joy come from within, not from anything in the physical world. There is such joy for those who can focus on listening to good music, gardening, reading, having a delicious lunch with a beloved friend or an interesting new acquaintance. Our thoughts and emotions must be guarded with such discipline that we never allow fear, anger and other negative emotions to enter the inner citadel of our consciousness and destroy our peace and equilibrium.

How comforting it is in times of stress to be able to look within your secret self and realize that you have everything you need for complete joy and happiness. Do not allow anything outside your universe to become so important that it can destroy your inner harmony. How powerful fear and anger are, and how destructive!

If we can face it, we will realize that negative emotion has no power of its own, only the power we give it. We give it power by our reaction to it. The same situation may exist in the lives of two different people. One person will not be affected by it at all if the emotion is transmuted through understanding. The other person, in fear, may react with emotion strong enough and powerful enough to kill.

I can thank my dear friends for teaching me a very valuable lesson. Being human, I am not always in control of my thoughts, and I can suddenly realize I have opened the door and let in some destructive enemies. I try to be vigilant in my practice of watching those negative thoughts that go galloping through my head, and I often catch the rascals before they get too far. If caught in the act, I can throw them out before they have done much harm.

We must remember that our world is comprised of thought, and we are constantly building or destroying in every second of our lives by what we are thinking and feeling. It is the feeling or emotion that has the power to build or destroy. Be alert, be on guard and march bravely into the veiled future.

35

Judgments

*O*n my early years in Sedona there was a little restaurant in old uptown called Paula's Goldust Café
where the flower children and hippies hung out each
day. I don't believe that is what you call a young group
of New Agers now, but that was what they were labeled
back thirty years or more ago. My real estate office was
just up the street, and I often went to the Goldust Café
for breakfast or coffee. The air would be full of the
smell of pot and a bit heady, to say the least. I was one
of the very few so-called members of the establishment
who went into that place.

The young people would glance at me as I came in
wearing my high heels, elegant clothes and the latest
hairdo. There were often a few sneers of contempt as I
walked by, because they had me pegged as one of the establishment — a very unpopular word in those days
among the New Age community.

One day I walked into the restaurant and saw that all

the booths and tables were taken. As I hesitated, one of the groups slid over and asked if I would like to sit with them, which I did. They began to take me to task and poke fun at me because I was one of the establishment. I listened politely for a while and finally said, "But I'm as much a hippie as you are. I am only disguised as a businesswoman because that is the role I decided to play to make a living in this lifetime. But it's only a facade — a part I am playing to the hilt with all the trappings."

They took a second look at me and after that they began to relax. They told me that they couldn't find jobs and had to live on welfare or food stamps because no one would hire them. Over the next few months (or was it years?) I began to point out that if I looked like they did, no one would come into my office to buy real estate from me. A little at a time I tried to hint that some of them needed to cut their long, greasy-looking hair a bit shorter. Others needed to clean themselves up. They seemed to take great pleasure in looking as disreputable as possible. I tried to suggest that they did not need to look like that to believe the way they did. They could be true to self and still look regular enough to get work.

Eventually, many understood that in spite of how I looked, I was really being true to myself just as they were trying to do, and they began to look upon me as a friend, enjoying my little charade of looking like the establishment. Some even cleaned up their own acts and got jobs. I had a chance to listen to what they had to say and see where they were coming from. Many were fighting back at a society that was trying to push them into tight little pigeonholes that had nothing to do with what they wanted to do with their lives.

204

Most hadn't found any solutions. They were just resisting, which really was not getting them anywhere.
Some of those hippies are still here in Sedona, but now
they would never be recognized as having been a part of
that phase. The majority have gradually integrated into
the stream of life, but they have inwardly hung onto
their hippie consciousness, which, by the way, had
much to say for itself. It was a revolt against parents,
schools and churches that were trying to force them
into a mold that did not fit. I say bravo to them!

Love and *light* — do these words sound familiar?
Many of today's New Age community use those words
glibly, sometimes rolling them off their tongues like so
many Hail Marys repeated over and over. Few actually
understand or know the importance of the words they
are parroting. I sometimes shudder when those words
are flung at me, knowing that it is just the "in" thing to
say, with no power of thought or comprehension behind
it. Some of these same persons can be found busily crit-
icizing or finding fault with friends, family, the "orthodox" community or their lovers. These actions are not
consistent with walking our talk.

We might remind ourselves not to be so smug, believing we are the so-called enlightened ones or that we
are among the "chosen" and consciously aware of the
Truth and probably are one of the 144,000. And do we
have the attitude that anyone who does not meditate,
chant mantras, use crystals ad infinitum are ignorant
and so far behind us spiritually they will never catch up
in this lifetime? If you listen, you will note that these
sentiments are often the theme of New Age conversation.

I would like to give you a parable to show the truth of
our judgments. Let us use the rosebush, which is the

most highly evolved among the flowers. This lovely bush has some very large, showy, beautifully mature blossoms on it. But look — some of its blossoms are only half open; others are buds in various stages of unfolding. Does the full-blown rose look down its flower nose at the other blossoms in different stages of development and feel itself superior because it was the first to bloom? Are not all the roses growing on the same bush or even on the same stem? Think about it.

We are all one. We came from the same source and are all developing in our own time on our own path. We can read, study, meditate and intellectualize until the end of time, but that is not where it's at. In every phase of our lives we must practice what we profess to believe and have reverence for all sentient beings, no matter where we think they are on the ladder of evolution.

And who are we to judge by appearances? A great heavenly being may have come into physical life just to experience the life of a drunk in the gutter or the life of a drug addict. We never know with whom we may be rubbing elbows, nor do we know another's destiny.

36

A Time to Plant

Time is actually speeding up, and we are fast approaching the time when we had better start learning to grow as much of our own food as we can in our own back yard. The WWII Victory Garden is going to be a popular item of conversation again, but now is the time to stop talking about it and get busy. Gardening is not only a great form of outdoor exercise; it is wonderful for meditation and relaxation. When you are out there in your little garden pulling weeds and tending the plants, you will feel very close to nature, to God and to the Earth.

Another plus is that you won't have to eat those grocery store vegetables that are radiated and polluted with pesticides, then sprayed with who-knows-what to keep them from spoiling. I know you are going to say, "I have no room to grow vegetables. My lot is too small."

Here is where I am going to blow your excuses to smithereens. I have been experimenting with growing vegetables in this arid land for over twenty years and am now living on a small lot with a tiny backyard area approximately 25' x 25'. This gives me about 625 square feet of space to work with. I have proven you do not need acreage. All you need is a small back yard, plenty of water, a minimum of hard work and lots of determination.

Ten years ago, when I moved into my humble little mobile on its own small lot, I was told by my neighbors, "You can't grow anything on this hard, rocky soil." I had suspicions that my lot had been squirted with poison to kill the weeds, because there were none. This seems to be a regular thing in most neighborhoods — you just have the weed man come around regularly and squirt his poison around your yard so you won't have to weed. Know you not that those very weeds can be good to eat and could save your life if you had no food? Besides, if you must pull them, it takes only a few minutes a day and the exercise is good for you. By poisoning your yard, you are helping to pollute the underground water you drink.

I am an old gardener and not easily discouraged, no matter the odds against me. I always go out and turn over the Earth and plant seeds no matter what the conditions are. So at least I had to give my new yard a try. The first fall, I collected all the bags of leaves I could get from my neighbors' deciduous trees, piled them all over my small plot and watered them when they seemed dry. Over the winter the leaves rotted and made good mulch. I also started my own compost pile behind my garage and put all garbage and grass clippings on it so I could build up my own mulch. In the spring I added ingredients that the soil lacked, such as nitrogen, gypsum and a few other things like lots of good horse manure and bags of mulch from the nursery. I rototilled the whole thing several times the first year to break up the hard soil and mix everything together.

The next year I didn't even spade it. I just raked the soil to disturb it enough to plant seeds, watered it well until things began to pop out of the ground — and presto, another lush garden was on the way. Another thing I did was to plant worms, because I didn't have any. Worms are important to aerate the soil and help it retain moisture. Now when I turn over a shovelful of dirt, it is a fisherman's delight because it is loaded with those wonderful red, crawly worms.

I had been used to a half acre to work with, so on my new mini farm I had to plot and plan how I could get the greatest variety of veggies on that little postage stamp of a garden. I came up with the idea of vertical farming. On three sides of the area I placed lattices for plants to climb on. You would be surprised how many plants you can coax to climb, thus saving space. They grow upward instead of taking precious ground space.

The next year I really outdid myself. I had always grown squash, but the vines sometimes grew twenty feet or more; obviously there was not enough room for squash. So I planted them at the foot of a trellis at the back of the plot, and when they grew beyond the trellis I fastened their tendrils to the juniper trees above them and they continued to grow toward the light. They climbed clear to the tops of the two junipers, and in late summer the squash were hanging high above my head in great profusion — a sight to behold.

A friend who is a professional photographer took some wonderful pictures that show what squash will do in limited space when they have something to climb on. When my friends bring out photographs of their grandchildren, I whip out my prints of these huge banana squash hanging from the trees, for in a way they are like my children. The one at the top of the tree was the largest — it was twenty-two inches long and weighed twenty-seven pounds.

I stashed my squash in a cool, dark place and they lasted until about May. Periodically I would cut one up and divide it with my neighbors and several appreciative friends. There was such a yield that I was able to supply them with squash from early fall all through winter. I gave them only to those who appreciated the difference between store-bought and my organic vegetables. There is a noticable difference.

By planting carrots, beets, chard, kale, onions and parsley in late July, I had vegetables all winter and in June had to dig up buckets of carrots and beets and cut

Mary Lou with her 27-pound squash and more squash growing in the trees.

Mary Lou's mini farm behind her house.

Basket of bounty from my garden.

chard to make room for a new crop.

I realize that many of you will read this and agree it is a great idea, yet do nothing, asserting, "We don't need to do it yet." I've got news for you. It's later than you think. Time is collapsing and things are happening at a faster rate — don't put it off or you may live to regret it.

If an old gal eighty-five years young can grow her own vegetables, so can you. Try it — you may come to love doing it, because while you're at it, you are tuning in to nature, listening to the birds, the sighing of the wind through the trees and truly appreciating your planet Earth. If you have never grown your own food, you can't imagine the excitement and satisfaction of watching it grow and how accomplished you will feel at harvest time. Your garden will become your most sacred sanctuary, and the Earth will bless you.

37

Musing about Food
and the Future

This story is not a pleasant one, but it has made a
deep impression on me and I am going to tell it
anyway. Usually we don't make changes in the way
we've always done things unless we have a good reason.
There is no incentive for change unless we are led to
find a better way because we have new information on
the subject. Specifically, I am writing about the slaughtering of animals for food. This is not just about killing
animals in an inhumane way; it is also about the possible harm done to our physical bodies when we eat the
flesh of these animals.

We know that many, if not all, so-called primitive
peoples view the animals they hunt and kill for food as
entities who sacrifice themselves to the weapons of the
hunter, and these animals are treated with great respect.
Oftentimes elaborate ritual and ceremony precede a

hunting party, and serious and thoughtful attention, praise and thanks are publicly offered to the spirit of a slain animal.

Our "civilized" way is totally different. Had I not had this called to my attention when I was in my early teens, I might not be writing this now.

When I was a young girl living in Waitsburg, Washington, I often took long walks that led me past a small slaughterhouse. In time I became acquainted with the owner of this business, and it was he who made me aware of some interesting facts about meat. I'd always had difficulty eating meat, and as I listened to him I began to understand one of the reasons why. Later in my life I found out that I'd spent many lifetimes in India, where almost everyone is a vegetarian.

My newfound friend at the slaughterhouse told me that cattle are aware they are going to die (or that something is wrong) forty-eight hours before they are killed. He said they cry constantly those forty-eight hours because they are nervous, uneasy and terrified. Pigs also are intelligent animals and suffer fear before they are slaughtered.

This fear causes an acid in their flesh that makes it more difficult for us to digest. It seems a lamb is so innocent that if it has not been mistreated, it skips happily to the area of slaughter, with no fear. Chickens, turkeys and fish do not go into great fear, either. I guess their intelligence level is low.

Could this acid flesh be the reason many nutritionists now are recommending we eat chicken, turkey and fish instead of red meat? I suspect not. Their concern probably has to do with the steroids and other substances given to cattle to make them grow faster and larger so they will bring more profit in the marketplace.

I had studied and taught about the acid effect on the flesh of slaughtered cattle for years before I ever heard of steroids, and I still think there is much truth in what the man at the slaughterhouse told me. Perhaps the fear and terror felt by slaughtered animals resonates somehow in the human psyche, creating potential imbalances that stress the human metabolism.

In the decades ahead, perhaps we humans will have ongoing extraterrestrial contact with other civilizations in our galaxy. Recently I have read that the Pleiadians' diet is mostly fruit and vegetables, and they have no need of a complex digestive system as we do. If this is true, it's not too wild to wonder if one day humans might develop bodies that do not require food as we know it. Oh yes, this idea stretches the imagination, but if it should come to pass, we would no longer be slaughtering animals for food and ingesting fear-filled meat.

Or perhaps as time goes on and we learn more about nutrition and about other life streams, a change will come about in our culture's eating habits. We may eat less meat, and maybe animals being raised for consumption will be treated with love and respect and their death will be painless and free of fear. Perhaps people will understand that the feelings an animal had when it was killed for food are important to their own health.

I look forward to the time when food animals will be raised by sacred ranchers and farmers who make certain the meat they sell is not tainted with fear and terror or unnatural substances. Then it will be possible once again to eat meat that will benefit us. By that time we'll be able to live longer and healthier lives.

38

In the Now

One Christmas, on a trip home from Mexico after a visit with my family, I had an experience that set me to contemplating the real meaning behind the much-talked-of-and-written-about subject, "living in the now."

As I boarded the plane and found my seat, I became lost in thought about some of the incidents that had transpired among my family members during the holidays. A few minutes later my deep study was interrupted by a tap on my arm from a small boy across the aisle. He was about six or seven, with big brown eyes and dark curly hair. He said, "Part of your seat belt is on the floor and the Fasten Seat Belt sign is on." I thanked him and buckled up, noticing that he was also checking the person behind him and in front of him. He was one of those youngsters one might refer to as bright-eyed and bushy-tailed, aware of everything that was going on around him. I lapsed back into my reverie when I felt another tap on my arm. "Your glasses are on the floor and somebody might step on them," was his comment.

I decided I must really be "out of it" and began to focus on what was going on around me. I could see that about 90 percent of the passengers were preoccupied and deep in thought, or just out of it as I had been. When the plane took off, very few were aware of its lifting off the ground. They were lost in a book or magazine.

Looking again at the child across from me, I realized how alive he was, completely aware of what was happening inside as well as outside the plane. He wasn't missing a thing. His glance was taking in the landscape sliding by the windows on both sides, and he was obviously thrilled with the feeling of the great mechanical bird lifting off the Earth and hurtling into the clouds. His excitement was catching. I too began to thrill at that incredible moment of take-off that I had experienced many times before, and I realized this little boy was living totally in the now. At his age he had very little past to pull him backward, and for him, tomorrow or next week were certainly of no concern.

If you watch children at play, you will see they are completely immersed in the feeling, emotion and activity they are involved in, truly living the moment to its fullest. I began to think of one of Christ's teachings: "Unless you become as a little child, you cannot enter the kingdom of heaven." Was this what he was trying to tell us? To experience the present moment as though this moment is all there is? To take no thought of tomorrow?

This instant really is all there is — the only thing you can count on as reality. We go through life being only partly here, dwelling in the past or worrying about the future, missing the wonderful experience of what is going on around us right now — the sounds, the smells, the clouds forming in the sky, the wind ruffling our hair, the interesting expression on the face of a passerby. Because of our reverie, we are only partly alive in this wonderful time, this wonderful body, this glorious day.

Life is now. It exists only in the present moment. Thoughts that are projected toward the past or future are actually cheating you, limiting your experience of present time and also draining you of your precious energy and vital expression. In whatever activity you engage, be it the most humble or menial task, try practicing being there fully in consciousness. This is being in the Presence of God, thus being fully alive.

Move into each new day with the faith of a child, meeting every moment with the joy of just being alive, aware of all the delicious and interesting things going on around you, accepting it all with no judgment, no tension, completely relaxed and ready for whatever comes.

As you practice the Presence as often as you can, you will find deep fulfillment in simply doing what is required of you in the moment. All that is real in your life will remain, and all that is unreal will just melt away.

39

When Hearts Are Troubled

When our hearts are troubled and we need the comfort of a deep spiritual faith and something to hold onto, many of us are now turning to mantras, affirmations, chants, crystals, medicine wheels and so on for healing and peace of mind. I have used all these things and acknowledge their value in times of stress. But the one help that has worked best for me and has saved my sanity in times of trouble has its roots way back in my childhood — the familiar old Twenty-Third Psalm.

My parents divorced when I was about nine years old, and for a time my family was scattered to the four winds. I considered myself the fortunate one because I was left with an uncle and aunt who owned a large sheep ranch in eastern Washington. There I was soon immersed in the lives of thousands of sheep and their sheepherders. In fact, occasionally I was sent out with a band of sheep, a wise old sheepdog and a gun on my hip — quite a responsibility for one so young. This happened during a time when most of the sheepherders were caught up in a flu epidemic. Miraculously, I had been spared the illness.

The shepherds were mostly Basque, a strange and silent breed, totally dedicated to caring for their flocks of sheep. I soon discovered why the Bible often uses sheep, especially lambs, as the symbol of trust, faith and innocence.

Sheep are completely dependent on their shepherd to keep them from harm and find them food. As I grew to understand the ways of sheep and their herders, I began to gain an intimate understanding of the Twenty-Third Psalm, and it became a very important part of my life. I would like to give you an interpretation of it from the viewpoint of my experience.

The Lord is my shepherd; I shall not want. The sheep have no fear of lack or want because they have total faith in their shepherd.

He maketh me to lie down in green pastures. He leadeth me beside still waters. He restoreth my soul. A good shepherd leads his flock into green fields where they may eat their fill and lie down to rest in the shade. He is careful that they do not overeat because sheep bloat easily on green grass. He also knows that a sheep will drown in swift waters because their wet wool will pull them down, so he takes them to a little backwater pool in the river where they can drink in safety.

He leadeth me in the paths of righteousness for his name's sake. The shepherd leads his flock over safe paths and avoids the steep and rocky places.

Yea, though I walk through the valley of the shadow of death, I will fear no evil; for thou art with me; thy rod and thy staff, they comfort me. When a shepherd takes his sheep through dangerous valleys and canyons where there are predators and obstacles that could cause them harm, they have such faith in their ever-present shepherd that they have no fear. The "rod and staff" is a long staff with a crook at the end of it, which the shepherd uses to pull them back to safety if they wander too close to a cliff or get caught in a bramble bush. He gently extricates them so that no harm comes to them, and he chases away the coyotes that often follow the herd to look for a fallen animal.

Thou preparest a table before me in the presence of mine enemies. Thou anointest my head with oil; my cup runneth over. Surely goodness and mercy will follow me all the days of my life, and I will dwell in the house of the Lord forever. At eventide the shepherd drives his flock into a fenced enclosure where he is camped. He knows they will be safe for the night while the predators look on, and he gives them everything they need for their safety and comfort. He feeds them a little grain and goes among them looking for those who have sustained a cut or abrasion. He tenderly anoints the sore spots with oil and gives them their fill of water from a spring or trough.

If only we could be as trusting of our Lord as those precious innocent sheep who rely totally on their shepherd as their savior, we would surely move without fear through all kinds of trials and tribulations.

If you memorize the Twenty-Third Psalm and slowly repeat it over and over as you go to sleep, thinking each phrase through as you go along, feeling the same kind of faith and trust as a sheep feels in the presence of his shepherd, you will find that muscles in your neck, your back and your whole body go limp and relaxed as you give over your cares and anxieties to your personal

Shepherd. You will drift into sleep with the utmost confidence that your problems will somehow be solved and that someone is loving you and watching over your life. Try it; it works.

40

Attitude

*O*f I've learned nothing else in my many years in Sedona, I've learned that whatever happens in one's life is really of no consequence. The thing that really matters is what your attitude is regarding the event. As someone has said, an attitude of mind is the most important part of what happens. Every experience you have gone through in this lifetime was given to you so that you might learn a valuable lesson, and if you will look closely at each happening and try to understand what you were to learn from it, life will become an interesting game instead of being a life full of traumatic emotional ups and downs. There is nothing wrong with the human race except destructive emotions.

Again I say, *the important thing is not what happens to you, but what your attitude is toward what is happening.* If you can remember this, your life will be less difficult.

The chemistry of your body, affected as it is by emotional states, is very delicate. Self is subject to thousands of influences, most of which you are completely unaware of unless you can become the witness and watch someone close to you. Notice how that person is physically affected by outside influences as well as by personal emotions. Then you will be more aware of how your own body reacts to everyday influences. Noises, newscasts and even smells are constantly affecting your health, as are your thoughts, emotions and feelings.

The greatest thing to help oneself is the habit of being in the Presence of God and being constantly alert to your attitude toward everything that is happening in your life. Ask yourself constantly throughout the day, "What am I to learn from this occurrence in my life?" Nothing is too small to overlook because everything is a learning. Assume the attitude of gratefulness for your opportunity to learn another valuable lesson, be it ever so small. This attitude takes the sting out of life and gives you a feeling of accomplishment when you can look back and see that five years ago you could not have handled the incident as well as you can now. At every turn of the road, if your attitude was right, you gained a step forward on your path to enlightenment.

Snatch moments. Invent reminders. Post sentinels in your mind until this divine habit of watching your attitudes becomes a constant way of being. It is rather humiliating to find how seldom we are masters of our minds. Who does not know the temptation of yielding to an emotional upsurge that hardens first into a destructive thought and is so swiftly followed by the spoken word?

Make your life a high adventure with each delay, each disappointment, simply a meaningful hurdle, another challenge on your way to attainment.

226

41

Value of Words

Back in 1991 many of us observed, with no small alarm, the possibilities of a world war and economic chaos, and we're still doing it. We realized that the year ahead could be fraught with some very difficult times. In listening to all the psychics, prophets and those full of negative predictions, we could easily feel that there might be some truth in all those gloomy forecasts. It would have been so easy to sink into fear and apprehension.

The gloom merchants are still with us, spreading uncertainty and alarm around the world. So what to do? We can either go down into the pit of despair, or we can pull our forces together, tighten our belts and face whatever happens with goodwill and cheer, realizing that all prophecies do not come to pass.

We chose this dream. We even helped to write the scenario, and now is the time to face the consequences. Together or singly we can make a difference by carrying the light into the dark abyss when humankind finds itself wallowing in despair.

I keep remembering an old hymn from long ago, "Brighten the Corner Where You Are." The way ahead may be filled with danger and unknown terrors, but we can lighten our own little corner wherever we may be and thus help those around us to march on into whatever is ahead with courage and strength.

I once attended an all-day workshop in Phoenix where Arthur Fanning channeled a great entity called Atlanto. Arthur was helping us open our chakras and expand our consciousness. Atlanto was similar to the early Ramtha and took a personal interest in each person attending Arthur's popular sessions. (Now Arthur lives nearby in Cornville, giving weekend seminars and channeling information from Jehovah and Yahweh.)

We were doing a mind-expanding exercise that pulled our attention to the vibrational value of words on our whole being. There we were, all lying on the floor, relaxed, with minds at peace, when we were instructed to listen carefully to the words Arthur would speak. We were to note how the emotional impact of each word traveled down into the body and what organs were affected. Some of the words were: sex, work, God, joy, ecstasy, dog and so on. He watched the auric changes around our bodies as we absorbed the spoken words.

Interestingly enough, the word that hit us the strongest was "work." Apparently we reacted negatively to that word. As you might imagine, the words "joy" and "ecstasy" brought wonderfully warm feelings and body vibrations that were healing and harmonious. Atlanto was showing us how important sounds and words are to our mental and physical health as well as our general well-being.

We learned that in order to stay on an even keel and help those around us to remain positive and cheerful, we must become aware of the potential of words to either hurt or heal and to choose our words wisely and carefully. It was a valuable lesson to become aware of what we say to others so that our words will not make matters worse, but will be a blessing and a morale lifter. Once a word is spoken, it cannot be taken back.

The world will need a lot of bright little corners as we move into the next century, so brighten your corner wherever you are!

42

Truth

My life has been one long search for the Truth, the reality of God that underlies the material world. My truth did not suddenly come to me in instant enlightenment. I had to search for years and dig deep, and I am still finding answers.

Having become disillusioned with Christian churches, I began to study the major religions of the world and found they all shared the same theme, mainly *Do unto others as you would have them do unto you.* I began to see this same truth in ancient philosophies. All the great teachers, saints and gurus have the same basic truth running like a golden thread through their teachings. All of them speak of surrender to the will of God.

But modern New Age teaching, which is pouring out in thousands of books and magazines, instructs us to be creators and make things happen in the way we desire. In this teaching our goal is to learn to manipulate and manifest what we want in the material world. Many people do this by nature and need no coaching. This philosophy seems to be in direct opposition to the less aggressive path of letting go and allowing God's way to be our guide.

For a long time I floundered about between these two paths. I proved to myself that, yes, I could alter circumstances. Often I could make things happen. After some time and much in-depth contemplation, I realized that what I wanted and willed to happen was not necessarily God's will, nor was it best for my growth and well-being. I began to go back to the old teachings based in antiquity. Even the Lord's Prayer says, "Thy will be done."

Mother Mira, who presided over Sri Aurobindo's ashram for fifty-six years and lived to be ninety-five, was a master of surrender to the Lord, whom she spoke of as the Divine. From the time she was a child, her entire life was spent in search of God, and the last fifty years of her life she practiced surrendering not only her mind and soul, but also the very cells of her body to the Divine. She worked at it day and night until the very end of her life.

Her agendas, and several books written since her passing by her most devoted disciple, Satprem, have been a source of inspiration to me for the last twenty-five to thirty years. Satprem's latest books, *The New Species*, *Mind of the Cells* and *Life without Death* are among the most challenging and informative I have ever studied.

The dichotomy of working for millennia to build the ego and the self-will, with the goal of finally becoming strong, dominant and self-willed as a finished product, is strange food when we are also working to let go and let God take over! But to graduate from humanhood and move on to be a "supramental being" (a complete new species), according to Sri Aurobindo, one must drop all ego completely, let go of self-will and surrender to God's will.

What a complete reversal of what we have been doing for eons! It is not easy to change. I am still struggling every day, every minute, wondering how long it will take me to break the old habits of self-will and the falsehood of worldly beliefs, for they are so deeply embedded in the very consciousness of my cells.

To do this you must live a normal life, for it is life itself that provides at every instant the opportunity to measure your progress. You can renounce the world and live in a cave or sit on a mountaintop giving full surrender to God, but there will be no circumstances to test you. This is not a true surrender because when you come back from your isolation, you will find you must start all over again. Growth takes place in the very soil of your daily life.

At one time I studied phrenology, a science of the external shape of a person's skull, the bone structure of the head, the size of the nose, chin and so on. This was a fascinating study. I have noticed many strong, dominant faces, especially here in Sedona. Many of these people are here to graduate. These faces usually consist of a large nose and mouth, strong chin and cheekbones, prominent forehead and large, forceful eyes — a real take-charge kind of person.

I realize these people have been working for millions of lifetimes to achieve their strength of self-will. How could one ever say to them, "Now you must give it all up and surrender to God — 'Thy will, not mine!'" No doubt these compelling individuals have been manipulating circumstances and those around them for some time and serve as leaders in some capacity. This type of person truly is needed at this time because so many people are weak, vacillating and in need of leadership.

These strong, forceful, take-over types have an important place in our society, but what would happen if they were to give up self-will and give up to God? It is my belief that they would become human dynamos — still leaders, but coming from a completely different direction.

I have been privileged to know a few, very few, of these highly evolved people who have given up to God. It is not easy. The process itself is simple, but very difficult to do. Our old way of thinking and our old ingrained habits go so very deep. When I meet people who have done this, I feel tremendously humble and appreciative of the sacrifice they have made of their human will and strength, a magnificent happening. In the future I believe we will see many more of these beings, because as Mother Mira has said, "Be careful, I am catching. This surrender can be highly contagious because we are all One."

This kind of surrender does not mean becoming a wimp or a doormat. You are surrendering to God, not to man. You become even stronger in the newfound strength of God. Even your physical body follows and is uplifted because there will be a change in the very consciousness of your cells: They will begin to fill with light.

43

The Falsehood

*A*fter publishing an article about some of the outstanding healers who have come in (and out) of Sedona as well as some who live here now, I received a stack of thoughtful comments from readers. One person wanted to know why her friend could be healed while she herself did not have any results.

Having been vitally interested in all manner of healing over the years and having sampled the work of every healer who came to Sedona and observed the results, I too have asked myself this same question. Of course we can always blame our karma, a much-used and -abused word these days. Another person commented, "Why would a loving Father God want us to suffer in this life for some mistake made in a past life?"

My answer to both of these sincere questioners is that our loving Father God surely does not want us to suffer for past mistakes, but He has given us free will (the ability to make our own choices), and this is where we run into the major problems in our lives. It is we who are our own judge and executioner. Deep in our subconscious we may have a strong remorse or guilt that does not allow us to be healed. We believe we are not worthy and don't deserve to be healthy. This unconscious belief often denies us love, prosperity and other pleasures and comforts in our lives.

I have often observed certain people being cured instantly of some terrible disease. Obviously they had decided deep down inside that they had paid enough for past errors and mistakes and were ready to accept the healing. While this is true for many, I have noticed that over time the illness may return to some who have experienced a healing. In these situations it would appear that the persons involved were not able to sustain and hold their healings because of a negative thought pattern or because the cause of the difficulty had not been remedied.

For millennia we have been programmed and brainwashed to believe in sin, guilt and punishment. Gradually we grew to believe in these negatives. I call these beliefs *the Falsehood.* You might call it the devil, the dark forces or the Antichrist, it makes no difference. It is all the same thing, and it rules our lives according to the belief or strength that we give it.

I firmly believe that if we could really dig deep enough to rid ourselves of these falsehoods, there would be no more sickness or death. We can do this *mentally* through affirmations, meditation and prayer, but *emotionally* it is far more difficult. *Physically,* it is almost impossible, because the falsehoods have been impregnated into the cells of our bodies. The human being is enmeshed in the flesh of his body, and the flesh is very ancient.

Our body cells bear the stamp of race memories and experiences of past ages. This is why our tired flesh has met with savagery, war, sorrow and grief and is so friendly with despair. It is because of all these cell memories that we find it easy to give in to disbelief and cynicism. I am sure that once we become aware of how firmly and completely the Falsehood has taken us over, we can start to let go of all the old habits and belief systems that obscure the light. With constant vigilance we can overcome the Falsehood.

This light is more powerful than the heavy race record that we carry in our cells. To move into the light means staying alert and aware of our every thought and emotion, every waking hour as best we can. This is practicing the Presence, knowing that God is the only reality and refusing to accept the old Falsehood so firmly entrenched in our being. To a diseased and unhappy soul, the offer of such peace and freedom seems almost impossible, almost a mockery.

We who are facing a world of unleashed savagery must plunge into the living Presence with courage and faith in the ever-present reality that these are forces beyond our understanding. We can become stronger in our realization of the immortality within us as each day we take another step toward the total rejection of Falsehood.

Yes, I believe that even the so-called law of karma is part of that great Falsehood and can be shed in an instant if we could only grasp the significance of Truth. This is something that can be obtained in a sudden blinding flash of realization in one lifetime, or it can take years of patient denial of Falsehood, plodding along day by day and replacing every negative thought, emotion and act with positive thoughts of Truth, catching ourselves in the act of accepting another false belief. This is the way most of us have to do it.

Why not stop yourself each day when you find you are accepting negative beliefs about lack, ill health, old age and death? Why not say to yourself, "No, I will not accept that negativity. It is part of the Big Falsehood"? If you can do this and cancel out the negative beliefs, you will find yourself feeling lighter and things going easier. Eventually it will be a way to total enlightenment, which is the true path to God.

44

Time to Let Go

When the old Keller Building was reduced to a pile of rubble several years ago, I was asked by many friends if it gave me sorrow to see it go. It had been the center of many interesting and exciting happenings during the thirty-one years I was in the building, and I have fond memories of what went on there, especially of the many gifted healers, speakers, psychics and channelers. Many great ones have graced the building with their presence during those years.

Fortunately, I was able to completely let go and relinquish that phase of my life with no pangs of sorrow or regret that it was over. I felt that it was an era that was finished, and all that is left are heart-warming memories of those who came and for a time honored us with their wisdom, knowledge and gifts of the spirit. I could write volumes about many of those personalities. I have written about some of them in this book and enjoyed every colorful memory.

So the old Keller Building is gone, and in its place stands the beautiful Hillside Court. Life moves on and on.

Mary Lou's favorite car, a lavender dune buggy with purple upholstery, in front of the old Keller Building.

45

Golden Years

I have heard so many young people comment that they fear and dread old age. They are relating to typical elderly persons who have been put into a retirement home and sit by the hour in a wheelchair, waiting for the end.

Your latter years do not need to be this way. They can be peak years of much freedom, peace and accomplishment. Sedona has some prime examples of this. I call them jewels in Sedona's crown. They range in ages between seventy-five and one hundred and three, and are active, independent and busy, not only enjoying life, but making valuable contributions to the community. To name a few: Iris Clark (teacher, writer and forever young), Lehmann Hisey (brilliant academic) and Dr. Francis Houston (healer and herbalist), all creative and involved in their chosen work.

Many Sedonans fondly remember Dr. Mary Stevens, Doc Bill Brown, White Bear and Naomi Fredericks.

These four "jewels" recently passed on, each one leaving a special impact on Sedona. Did you know that the artwork on the walls in Emile's popular **Coffee Pot Restaurant** was done by White Bear when he was in his eighties?

There are many others, some I do not know personally, who are quietly, with no fanfare or theatrics, living a fruitful and fulfilling life, spreading their love and knowledge wherever they go. It is true they may have their health problems, an ache here and there, a slowing of their steps, but their minds are still active and productive and they continue to push the frontiers of their minds out beyond the ordinary. Their spirits are young and vibrant, and I salute them and am proud to be in their company.

I'd like to give you some of their secrets. First, for what it is worth, none of them are vegetarians. They eat rather sparingly, small portions, but eat what they want and seem to enjoy food. I consider them all highly evolved individuals, so what does this tell you about vegetarianism? They have learned not only what is best to do, but most importantly what not to do. They are no longer naive and gullible — they have a fine-tuned discernment and can spot a phony a block away.

Most of those in their golden years have let go of a lot of unnecessary things that held them down in their younger days. We have all accumulated a large bag of garbage over the years, starting early in our youth. These consist of fears, hurt feelings, angers, resentments, unresolved differences with family and close associations and countless negative opinions as well as a preoccupation with "what will the neighbors think?" We keep stuffing this junk into our bag and dragging it along with us while it grows heavier and heavier. Do we really need all this stuff?

At some point, usually in our later years, we begin to take a good look at the contents of our garbage bag and make an effort to get rid of some of it. From this point on, the older we get, the more of it we take out and leave behind, making the weight lighter and lighter. Each lightening of the load gives us more freedom and allows our energy to be used for more important issues.

Even a lot of those superfluous desires, once held so dear, have been eliminated, because somehow they seem rather unimportant when put under the magnifying glass of reality. Some of the useless activities that involve striving to do what others expect of you also get tossed out. As the load you have been dragging along for years becomes lighter, you have more time for yourself and for contemplation, which is the highest form of meditation.

No longer do you allow anyone to pressure you into doing things that are not of your choosing. Now you follow your inner guidance. In other words (this may sound selfish but is actually highly productive), you now have time to be *you*. You become mellow and less critical of others and see the happenings around the world as part of a larger plan.

Hopefully, you have learned true compassion as well as the ability to allow others to be themselves. And another big plus is that you have learned not to get involved in the problems of others because you now understand the need for everyone to learn life's lessons the hard way just as you had to. You can actually interfere with another's karma by being overly helpful. With advancing years, you learn how rewarding it is to have your younger friends seek you out for your advice and opinions because they know that wisdom and experience usually accompany age.

Because you are less tense and ambitious, you have time to smell the roses, watch a sunset or stop and listen to the song of a bird. It can be a lovely and fulfilling time of life if you allow it to happen gracefully and serenely.

One last comment that is really important: Recently I have met more and more young people in their thirties, forties and fifties who have wisdom beyond their years. This gives me hope for the future of the human race. In this fast-paced Aquarian Age, the young do not have to wait for old age to be wise and discerning.

46

Joy and Reverence

*L*et us always greet the future with confidence, great courage and joy, remembering that we chose to be here at this momentous time. Never allow the prophecies of darkness and destruction to fill you with fear and trepidation. Do not permit the crepe-hangers, who see the future only in terms of obstacles and disasters, to make you stumble. March forward and do not let the negative news creep under your shining raiments of light. Truth will shine in dark places, and out of seeming chaos you will see the hand of God working. As you move into this exciting time of destiny, be of good cheer and meet it with a joyful, expectant heart.

Let worship and reverence for all things be a part of every thought and act in your daily life. You can hold this goal subconsciously while occupied with the humdrum activities of everyday living. Occasionally pause throughout the day to check your thoughts and attitudes. Where are you at this moment in time? Are you in a state of lethargic ignorance, full of tension and heaviness, or are you reaching upward, purifying your total nature through your listening spirit?

Many years ago (it could have been at least forty years), one of the many gurus who have come and gone in Sedona was often seen walking down the street, stamping his feet as he walked. *Stamp! Stamp! Stamp!* Sometimes when sitting at a table or desk, he would strike his hand forcefully against it. *Bang! Bang! Bang!* Eventually I asked him to explain why he did this. He said it was to keep himself constantly *aware of the moment* in his body. He was making each moment more real so he would not lapse into the half-conscious state one often slips into during a typical day.

I felt there was some merit to what he was saying. Try practicing being consciously aware of each moment. There is only *now*, but if you are not on your toes, you will miss the moment and lapse into the sleep of forgetfulness, which I like to term "the walking dead."

Use your indwelling spirit. So often we pray to spirit and then go about our affairs under tension, taking upon ourselves the burden from which we have asked to be freed. There is no fear of death and calamity for those who walk the path as christs of that angelic order that leads men back to their lost knowledge of divinity. There is no fear of circumstance as we gain mastery and perform wonders. We achieve this through our thoughts as we let God indwell and surcharge our entire being.

Never let yourself be swept into the outer circle of thoughts of resentment, foreboding, pride and fear, for these negatives will pull you down. Step back, sit down, and a table will be set before you in the presence of those enemies.

Rest with your whole mind and soul on the surety of the Shepherd's guiding hand. Follow happily through the valley of shadows. Follow with full trust. Bless each moment and purify it, and the negativity will be removed. Pressure will be lifted and doubt released, then you will indeed feel free. When you turn within to that eternal stillness, it is then that your cup runs over and spills itself into your universe. You must remember your way back into the very center of your being, to that eternal fountain of refreshment within.

Give out love, give royally of it, but keep silent. You need not go about making a big display. Laugh and be merry, for that is healing to those who despair. Be humble and tender. Be selfless and patient and forgiving. Be simple. If you live like this in the midst of world upheavals and everyday confusion, you have nothing to fear. Keep yourself in the light within and you will have nothing to cause you to tremble and falter.

Welcome each morning with gladness and live every day with your banners of courage unfurled, your armor of light around you while you sound your *trumpets of joy*.

Final Word

Never Too Late to Learn

You might think that after eighty-five years on this Earth, I would have learned all my lessons. Not so! I swear I am still learning, still polishing new facets.

When I was eighty I had a stroke — a devastating and debilitating experience. How could this happen to me, who had tried to eat right, to exercise my body and to monitor my thoughts most of my life?

After many tests, which showed a 95 percent blocked artery, I was told I could have another stroke that would surely do me in for good.

My beloved niece Diana, who has always tuned in to me, suddenly arrived on the scene with no previous knowledge of my condition. The following morning, we were on our way to the Arizona Heart Institute in Phoenix, where I was scheduled for surgery on the carotid artery, the principal artery in the neck.

Diana smoothed the way for me by explaining to the

nurses and doctors that this was the first time her eighty-year-old aunt had been in a hospital, and that probably I would not understand all the procedures, so they must explain them to me. She stayed with me and oversaw everything, making sure things were being done right. She didn't leave until nine o'clock that night when they put her out. I don't know what I would have done without her. She had to leave town in a few days, but before she went she lined up a live-in nurse to take care of me.

At first I'm afraid I didn't handle the situation very well. I was really angry with my body for letting me down. I was also terribly upset when I was told it would be a long time before I could drive again, if ever. I hated being taken care of like the helpless convalescent that I was — I, who had always been so self-sufficient and independent. Well, I can tell you, I had quite a battle with myself.

When I began to show signs of a little improvement, I started to resent the fact that people were doing things for me that I felt I should be able to do for myself. Instead of letting go and accepting help, I would try to stagger to my feet and make an effort to do it myself. Repeatedly it was made clear to me that this was not going to work; I was too weak and unsteady. So I stewed and fretted and resented the assistance I was given. And this is when I began to learn big lessons.

I had lots of time to do nothing but think, and finally I realized that I might as well accept what had happened to me and be grateful for those who were trying to help. I can't say this was easy. At first I found it terribly humiliating to be helped to a chair, presented with a bowl of oatmeal and tied into a big bib because I was so sloppy and spilled everything. Also, I found it difficult to have people telling me what I could and could not do. This was a trying time, but it was also beneficial.

I began to understand that now was the time for me to remember lessons I had learned, professed to believe and had taught others over the past fifty years. Slowly, gradually, I began to get myself under control and realize this was a new ball game. I had to learn to be grateful for all the little things I *could* do instead of rebelling at what I couldn't do. If you don't learn this along the way, somehow life will manage to teach you in spite of yourself.

Even though my walking is unsteady and sometimes I use a cane, I have progressed to driving my car, doing my own errands and pretty much taking care of myself.

Perhaps the most rewarding part of this whole episode was finding out how many truly good friends I had — people who really cared about me, helped and encouraged me throughout the entire experience. I was amazed at those people, whom I didn't suspect were fond of me, who just turned up and did wonderfully thoughtful and caring things to help make life easier. One week three such angels (whom I never before had thought of as angels) appeared to assist me. No one asked them. They just came to my aid out of the goodness of their hearts. What a heartwarming revelation!

Looking back on all of this, I can actually say I am glad I had the opportunity to experience this most difficult time. I found out that at eighty years of age and even beyond, we can continue to learn valuable lessons. Because of the stroke, my life has completely changed. Now I am able to live each day with rejoicing for what I have and what I can do for myself, and I'm back on the positive path.

So much negativity is being expressed in our world today, if we allow it to slip through our defenses, we can be devastated. To protect ourselves from negativity, we must constantly watch our attitudes and be aware of how we react to what we hear and see. We must be watchful of our thoughts and attempt to concentrate on the hopeful and positive rather than dwelling on the negative. Sometimes I find it helpful to "fast" from television fare, the radio and the news and put my mind and thoughts on anything that isn't a downer.

At this time, our lives are the most complicated and challenging of any civilization on Earth. We need to be masters of ourselves as we wind our way through the darkness of horror and despair. Never lose sight of the fact that we are in the midst of a tight walk between the third and fourth dimensions. Many of the catastrophic events happening now need not affect us as long as we keep ourselves grounded and focused.

Allow me to remind you to move forward every day, shining your light on the negativity as well as on everyone you meet, and you will be a blessing to the world and to yourself. Let me repeat one of my favorite formulas for living: *Go forth seeing only beauty, and beauty will be upon your face.* When you persist in seeing only beauty, much of the negativity slips away.

My final words to you are, rejoice that you are living at this momentous time. Be one of those who is doing his share in helping to lift human consciousness toward the fourth dimension rather than joining the crowd that is dragging its feet. The latter group is insisting on staying in the third dimension and is listening to all the bleak and somber prophecies of disaster that attack us day and night.

You can make the choice to be a positive force in the world and sow seeds of hope and love and joy. This is your decision.

My Personal Prayer

The first thing in the morning and before

sleep at night, I ask that my heart chakra

be opened more each day . . . that I may

love as Jesus loves. I also ask that I may be

in the right place this day . . . doing

whatever God has for me to do . . . and

that I be an instrument of peace.

May All Blessings Be Yours

Map of Sedona

On the following five pages is the first published map of the Sedona red rock country and the information that accompanied it. Back in the '50s, Glenn Keller drew this map for our real estate business, and we had 10,000 copies printed. I still have some of them stacked in my closet. The general information was written by me.

Mary Lou

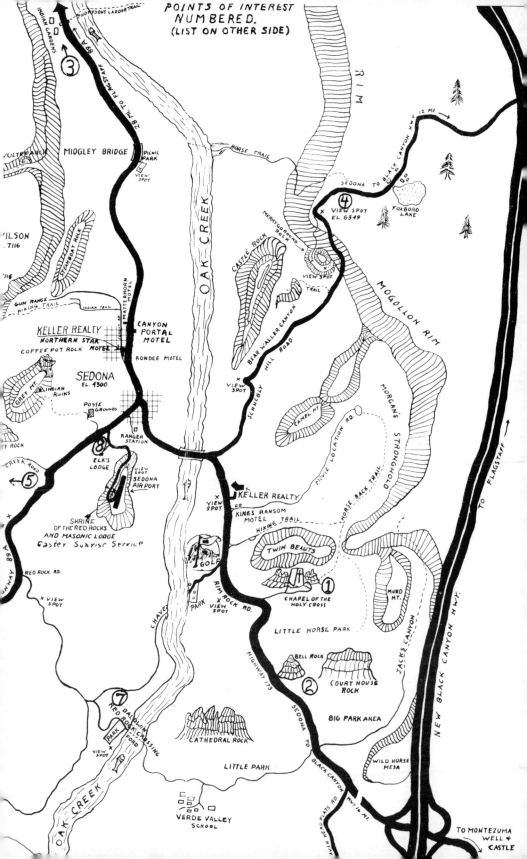

POINTS OF INTEREST
NUMBERED.
(LIST ON OTHER SIDE)

Points of Interest
Around Sedona

1. The Chapel of the Holy Cross.
2. Bell Rock and Courthouse Rock.
   (Background for many movies)
3. Drive through Oak Creek Canyon.
4. View spot at top of Mogollon Rim.
5. Drive through Boynton Canyon.
6. Devil's Arch, a natural bridge.
7. Picnic at Baldwin's (Red Rock) Crossing.
   (Don't forget your camera)
8. Pecos West wood carving.

CLIMATE
IN RED ROCK LAND

Spring (March-April-May) Average 71.3, average low 43.

Summer (June-July-August) Average high 92.0, average low 62.7

Fall (September-October-November) Average high 77, average low 49.3

Winter (December-January-February) Average high 55.6, average low 31

Average High For The Year 74.

Clear, Clean Fresh Air. Rain Fall 12 to 14 inches per year.

Oak Creek Canyon & Sedona nestles among red, towering cliffs. Its beauty is natural and unspoiled. Here there are good eating places and excellent accomodations in hotels and motels, plus trailer courts, picnic spots and campgrounds.

As Sedona's leading independent real estate agency, Keller Realty has helped bring together hundreds of buyers and sellers during our many years in business here.

Through our association with Previews, Inc., the national real estate clearing house, we offer a complete national real estate service. If you have property to sell or trade anywhere, or if you are looking for just the right property to buy we can help you.

We would be most happy to discuss your real estate needs with you in confidence.

KELLER REALTY
**Two convenient offices to serve you:
At the Fountain in Uptown Sedona
and next to the King's Ransom.**

One Day Trips from Sedona and Return

* * * * * * * * * * * * * * *

The Red Rock Country* Welcomes You To

RELAX in our friendly community.

PICNIC at famous Red Rock Crossing.

HIKE, jeep, or go horseback riding over interesting trails in the area.

EXPLORE ghost towns; old mine sites - a challenge to you rockhounds.

FISH in the trout-filled Oak Creek or nearby streams and lakes.

HUNT for big game in the wild Mogollon Rim country.

DRIVE north, south, east and west from Sedona through unsurpassed scenery.

REST and get away from it all in the clear air.

*Where the Desert and the Mountains meet.

WELCOME...

to SEDONA and
OAK CREEK CANYON

OAK CREEK CANYON and Sedona, located almost in the heart of Arizona on Highway 89A, is the most colorful and breathtakingly beautiful vacation and retirement spot in the U. S. A.

The great out-of-doors is the primary attraction of this still unspoiled playground. There is a sparkling stream winding through the spectacular red rock formations and cliffs and the lush green growth of Juniper, Arizona Cypress, Pinon Pine, Cottonwood, Sycamore and many other trees adds the perfect framing for the red and pink monuments which surround the area.

Deer, elk, antelope, mountain lion, and wild turkey provide sport for the hunter. For the fisherman the trout of Oak Creek are large and plentiful, and they know no season. Hiking, horseback riding, square dancing, rodeos, amateur theatricals are all a part of this fabulous country. There is good swimming in the many natural pools along the creek, as well as artificial pools. This is a photographer's paradise — be sure to bring your camera.

The movie companies have long recognized the spectacular beauty of this area and many productions have been filmed here.

Within a short drive one may see Indian cliff dwellings, visit the ghost mining town of Jerome, explore hidden side canyons, or stand in awe at the wonders of the Grand Canyon and the Painted Desert.

With an altitude of 4300 feet, Sedona and the Canyon have long summers with warm days and cool nights. Spring finds the hills aglow with wild flowers and cacti blossoms. Fall weather is warm and crisp with the Canyon ablaze with autumn color. The short winters are stimulating with an occasional touch of snow to add frosting to the red sandstone cliffs.

This is the sort of place you will come to spend a day or a week and want to stay forever.

Index of Place Names

List of Illustrations